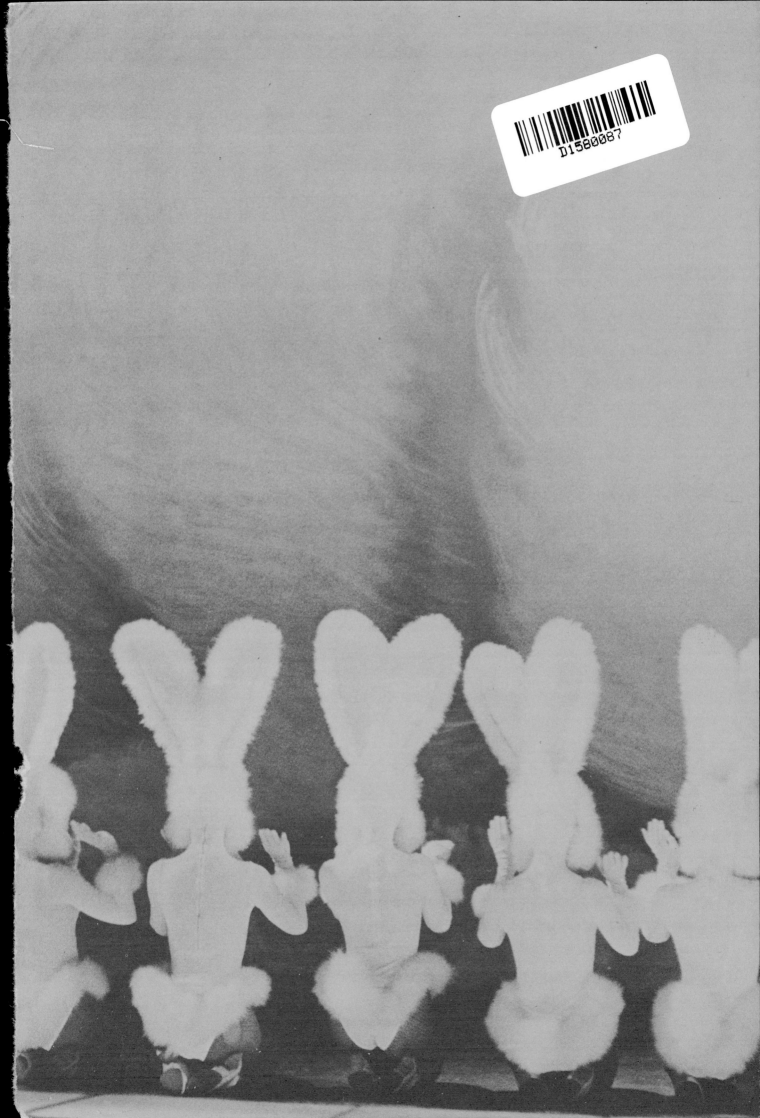

The Natural History of the

Chorus Girl

Derek & Julia Parker

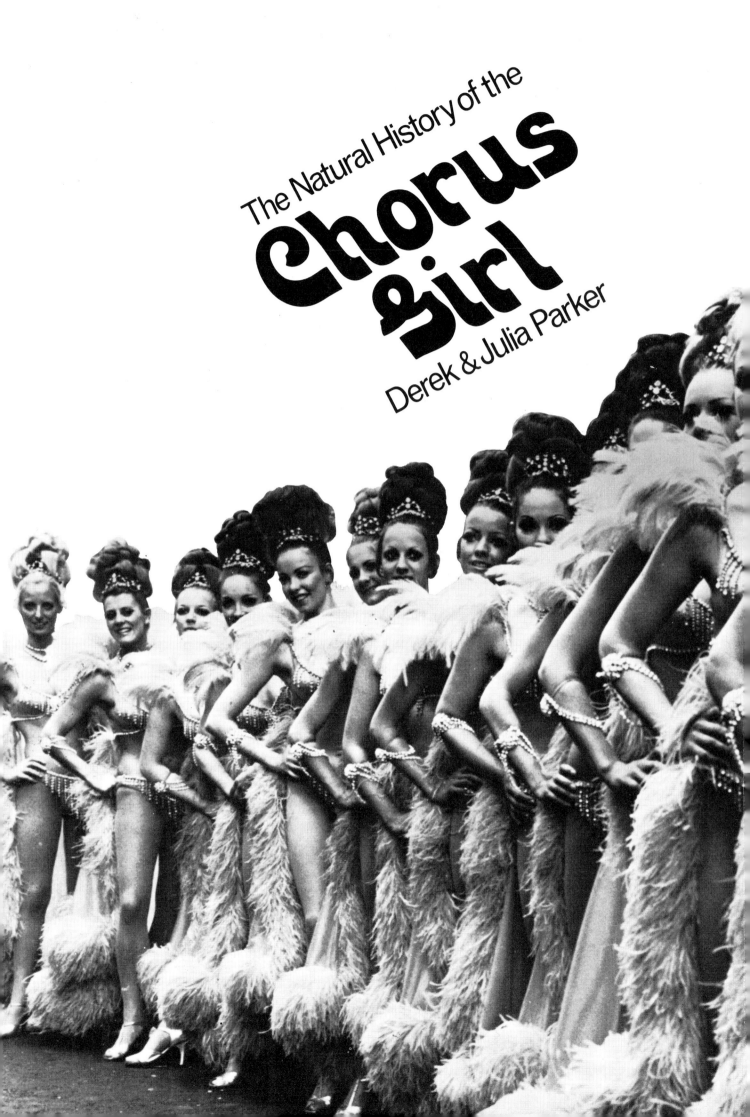

The Natural History of the Chorus girl

Derek & Julia Parker

David & Charles
Newton Abbot · London · Vancouver

In memory of
BILLY BELL
who we think
would have enjoyed
this book

Designed by Paul Watkins

Picture Research by
Anne-Marie Ehrlich

ISBN 0 7153 7076 6

Filmset by Keyspools Limited, Golborne, Lancs.

Printed photolitho in Great Britain by
Ebenezer Baylis & Son Ltd, The Trinity Press
Worcester & London for
David & Charles (Holdings) Limited
South Devon House, Newton Abbot, Devon

Contents

Introduction

Theatre historians may have a very strict notion of what they mean when they use the term 'chorus girl'. The public has never been so sure. If the theatre-goer of the turn of the century referred to a woman as 'a chorus-girl', he probably thought of the Gaiety Girl—but many of the beautiful young ladies of the Gaiety Theatre would have blushed with fury at the very idea. An American, in the 1920s, would have had a Ziegfeld Girl in mind; while in the 1870s in London, 'a chorus girl' would simply have been a lady who provided a comparatively stationary decoration on the periphery of a star's act. Earlier still, the girls of 'the ballet' would have filled much the same rôle that in the 1930s fell to the high-kicking Tiller Girls.

For the purposes of this book, which we hope is an entertainment as well as a ruminating history, we have purposely kept the definition as vague as possible: 'a chorus girl' to us means any young lady who, unnamed, has trod the boards in the company of her friends, providing a picture of feminine beauty for the delight of an audience of admiring men (and women, who always seem to have taken an almost equal delight in looking at beautiful girls).

This raises, one hopes temporarily, the spectre of the enthusiastic champion of Women's Lib who, protesting volubly (and properly) at the more unpleasant manifestations of beauty competitions, might perhaps feel that a girl should be ashamed at the very idea of being a chorus girl. Indeed, there might be something basically unpleasant in the idea if one were to assume that in some way the girls were offering themselves to the highest bidder, like so many legalised prostitutes.

In fact, that has almost never been the case. The chorus girl has only rarely, and individually, been as loose-living, and never as degenerate,

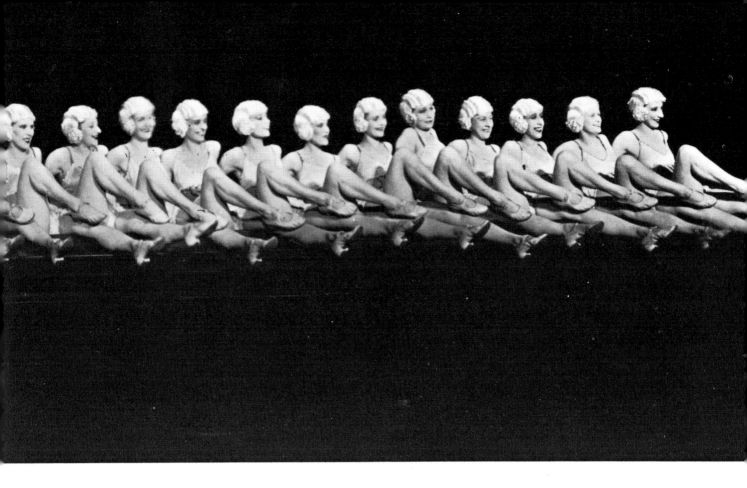

as popular fiction has suggested. More often than not, she has been a girl of no inconsiderable skill in dancing and/or singing, who has used that skill to make a living. Incidentally, she has almost always positively enjoyed showing herself off on a stage: the glamour of show-business has been in the limelight which has presented her as an object of admiration—evoking from the audience, the stage-door Johnny, 'the desire of the moth for the star'. But for the most part, she has found her twinkling to take far too much time and energy to permit her to spend any energy on affairs on the other side of the stage-door.

Our illustrations show how theatrical, but also personal, taste has changed. Some of the ladies in the earliest photographs would make a slim living these days, with their statuesque, monumental beauty, their thighs like tree-trunks. In other cases one can see just what their audiences saw in the girls' gaiety and charm.

Often, girls have of course stepped from the chorus into the centre of the stage, and have become stars: Jessie Matthews and Dame Anna Neagle, perhaps most famously, in England. When they do so, they step out of the pages of this book, which is a tribute to the chorus itself —to the girls who never saw their names in lights, who left the stage only for matrimony or retirement. We salute them, we remember them, we wish them well, those

dangerous, deplorable,
Bewilderingly adorable
Delightful dainty darlings of the chorus.

D. P.   J. P.

The Darlings of the Chorus

With lads who come from College,
    who've read the book of knowledge
(Except perhaps its most absorbing page)
Romantic education begins with gravitation
Towards the lovely sirens of the stage.
In years of indiscretion
We've had the same obsession
And frequently we get the craze anew,
They have a glamour that transcends
    the charm of other lady friends:
First of all 'tis Limelight lends
    enchantment to the view.
But when we see them closer
And hear them murmur 'Oh, Sir!
You're very kind and I don't mind
    provided I can bring a pal or two!'

We succumb to the craze
    for the nimble coryphées
Our elders and betters did before us,
We meet them, we treat them,
    we take them out to dine,
We pet them, we let them monopolise us.
Before very long we are going rather strong
Believing they honestly adore us—
The sympathetic strenuous excitable ingenuous
    engaging little ladies of the chorus.

To capture our affections
They alter their complexions
They're really most obliging in their way;
Your charming blonde of Sunday
    is my brunette on Monday
They find the more they please
    the more it pays!
And yet there's no denying
They can be rather trying,
But when the flashing eye is tear-bedewed
Swiftly will the laughter chase
    all shadows from the dimpled face
How the deuce can we keep pace
    with every changing mood?
Inconstant altogether
As charming April weather
But come what may they all display
A wonderful capacity for food!

With a smart pair of hose and a nicely powdered nose
And eyes that provoke and then implore us,
They fool us, they rule us
We never stand a chance!
They hoax us, they coax us . . .
 but there—God bless
All their dear little hearts
 if they don't aspire to 'parts'
Their faces and figures simply floor us.
Their witchery's continuous—
 The slender shapely sinuous
Enticing little ladies of the chorus.

The pert little flirts in abbreviated skirts
They drive us to drink but never bore us!
The dangerous, deplorable,
Bewilderingly adorable
Delightful dainty darlings of the chorus!

—Arthur Stanley
 (from *The Gipsy Princess*, 1921).

'We are sorry for you, Mabel Preston,' began Miss Wentworth, 'We are sorry for you, but you must get work elsewhere. We cannot have our nephew, Captain John Wentworth's shirts made by a ballet dancer. It would be setting a young man far too bad an example.'

Chambers' Edinburgh Journal, 1853

'A quiet fizz dinner' as seen by a nineteenth-century artist who took it for granted that the girls who participated in such riotous living must be 'ladies of the chorus'

1 The Rise & Fall of the Ballet Girl

Where does one start the story? When was the chorus girl born? The question is impossible to answer, partly because the definition of 'a chorus girl' has changed from time to time during the past century. *The Oxford English Dictionary* is uncharacteristically quiet about the origin of the term as applied to decorative young women, though the word 'chorus' itself was certainly in use in the seventeenth century (and derives from the Greek *khorós*, 'dance, band of dancers', referring to a band of interested spectators of the drama who danced and sang and otherwise took part in the performances).

But a young man striding purposefully down the Strand in the direction of Mr George Edwardes' Gaiety Theatre in the 1890s would have had a very different conception of a chorus girl than his counterpart in the 1920s or 1930s, on his way to a revue or a musical comedy. The tall, willowy, graceful, really rather remotely beautiful chorus girl of the Gaiety would not have recognised much kinship with the bright young thing of Mr Coward's revues.

The reason for the chorus girl's existence is not far to seek. Men have always taken pleasure in looking at girls, more or less clothed, more or less approachable. A glance at a Greek vase reveals what is a close relation to a chorus girl disporting herself around its bowl; the Egyptian equivalent of a chorus girl romps along the length of a wall-painting; girls prance through the frescoes of Indian temples, and enliven the façades at Angkor and Bangkok.

In primitive tribes, girls offer themselves to men in dance displays which are not too remotely connected with the ritual bouncings of the Young Generation, or even the high kicks of the Tillers. In fact, wherever a group of young ladies place themselves on view, emphasising their beauty by dance or pose, in or out of costume, the idea of the chorus girl is not too far away.

In the West, it is probably fair to begin the story with the nineteenth-century ballet girl who, far from being the highly-trained dancer of today's Royal Ballet, was a young lady whose expertise in the dance was peripheral to her personal beauty and vivacity, and whose morals were often no better than they should be. Just like the chorus girl of the Gaiety or of the Broadway musical, her main purpose was to attract. And attract she certainly did.

During the Regency and the reign of George IV, the ballet at the King's Theatre in the Haymarket, in London—the Italian Opera, as it was called—was the pleasure of the 'bucks' who during the intervals lounged conspicuously in the aisle (known on that account as 'Fops' Alley') and paid court to the ballet girls in the Green Room backstage.

Doubtless there were some wholly virtuous young ladies at the theatre; but one gets the impression that almost all of them took advantage of the tempting offers of 'protection' which were made them —for simple financial reasons. The chorus has always been under-paid. Some of the girls—like the notorious Louise Turner—altogether forsook the toil of the corps de ballet for an easier way of making a living, and for riches the stage was extremely unlikely to provide.

It was the adventures of the more notorious girls which provoked

such gossip in the outside world, and which tarred all 'theatricals' with the same brush. As has always been the case, those who did not enjoy the privilege of admission backstage imagined a much-exaggerated picture of immorality and debauchery.

'Of all the places for . . . downright laciviousness and intemperate intrigue, there is nothing in London equal to the King's Theatre,' wrote one moralist in 1830. 'Almost all the ladies in their turn fall victim to the Venus-like inspiration which hovers round and lives in the atmosphere of this Cyprian palace.'

Marguerite, Lady Blessington, Byron's friend, in her poem *The Belle of a Season*, found the front-of-house scene shocking enough:

Brisk music gayer scenes announces,
And in a half-dressed *danseuse* bounces
With arms that wreathe, and eyes that swim,
And drapery that scarce shades each limb,
And lip that wears a studied smile,
Applauding coxcombs to beguile,
As *entrechat* or *pirouette*
Doth 'Brava!' thundered loud beget.
When Mary saw her vault in air,
The snow-white tunic leaving bare
Her limbs—and heard the deafening shout
Grow louder as she twirled about,
With one leg pointed towards the sky
As if the gallery to defy;
Surprised, and shocked, she turned away,
Wondering how women e'er could stay,

And thinking men must sure be frantic
Who patronised such postures antic.
She felt abashed to meet the eye
Of every fop that loitered by:
And, oh! how rudely did it vex
Her fresh, pure heart to mark her sex
Thus outraged, while the noblest came
To gaze and revel in their shame . . .

Lady Blessington, if her tone of moral outrage seems a little forced, was in fact quite right; it was too often poverty that drove the ballet girl onto the stage in the first place, and then drove her off it into the arms of any man with money to spare. And to add insult to injury, English girls were not even permitted to show real accomplishment as dancers when they had it. Most of the leading dancers at the King's were foreign. A correspondent of *The Town* wrote in 1837:

'It is next to an impossibility for an English girl to
get engaged at the Opera in any other capacity than a
mere supernumerary or *figurante*; and while thus engaged,
she may be considered to be in an academy of whoredom,
for the Italian Opera, behind the scenes, is a perfect
seraglio for the use of the wealthy licentious . . . and
this is one strong indicative proof, that the patrician
patrons of that establishment seek but to put our
English girls to the vilest uses, while they enrich the
haughty Italians, French or German *danseuses* by the
most lavish presents and support.'

Opposite: A row of sedate but ingratiating Tanagra ladies of c. 250 BC from Canosa di Puglia, in Italy. Their entertainments may have been semi-private, but the atmosphere is that of the chorus-girl in her less vivacious moments

Above: A row of children diligently practising the fifth position in ballet, which they would demonstrate in pantomime for long hours and little reward

Not unnaturally, the loose morals of many of the girls at the King's gave the entire profession a bad name for their time; the general public never gave a thought to the fact that they were driven to prostitution by simple poverty. One distressed and respectable girl wrote to *The Era* in 1858:

'Because we wear short clothes, and show our
feet, which the Almighty gave us, we are pitied by the
most of our sex who sit in the front of a theatre, and
who are always very glad to look at us, although they
do think so badly of us; but I think if anyone will
seriously consider for a moment, they will come to the
conclusion that taking us as a body, and considering
the temptations to which we are exposed, we are not so
bad as we seem to be.'

But most respectable middle-class people regarded all ballet girls as little more than street-walkers. There is a revealing little scene in *The Ballet-Girl*, a short story which appeared in *Chambers' Edinburgh Journal* in 1853:

'The three old ladies gave each a little
scream.
"A ballet-dancer!" cried the eldest.
"With such short petticoats, Mabel!" said
Miss Silias reproachfully.
"Dancing in public on one toe!" exclaimed Miss
Priscilla, holding up her hands . . .
"We are sorry, Mabel Preston," began Miss
Wentworth, "We are sorry for you, but you must
get work elsewhere. We cannot have our nephew,
Captain John Wentworth's shirts made by a ballet
dancer. It would be setting a young man far
too bad an example." '

Not only polite society condemned these poor girls: shamefully, a Bishop of London actually refused a ballet girl the Sacrament, solely on the grounds of her occupation.

The idea of the chorus girl as a loose-liver survived well into the present century: poor girl, she has generally been far too tired after an evening's pelting up and down stairs to her dressing-room, changing her dresses, performing her routines, to be able to give much of her energy to living it up! The legend of 'availability' had been spread by prostitutes masquerading as 'actresses'—a habit which prevailed well into the twentieth century. But she has also been, from time to time, naive enough to provide easy meat for any manager whose own morals were not impeccable. Ignorant young girls from the provinces have always flown to London, to possible fame and fortune, at the drop of a pair of silk hose: in 1890 one of them wrote to the editor of *The Theatre*:

'Sir i take the pleasure in writing these few lines
to you please i write to ask you if you are in want
of a Girl for the stage i apply for it i am 17 years
of age and are a tall girl and have Been on the stage
twice Before i would be very Much pleased if you could
Assist Me in one i would be very Glad to come Please
would you be as kind as to write and let Me know.'

Even supposing that letters such as those reached wholly respectable managements, life upon the wicked stage was always full of opportunities for ruination. The nineteenth-century pornographic autobiographer, 'Walter', who has left such a vivid picture of his age, tells of a girl called Sarah, who was persuaded to go on a tour of France with a small chorus of dancing-girls:

'Everything went well at first, they made money,
then some of the troupe got discontented with their
share, quarrels arose, and two left, which spoilt the
tableaux. Then Mr Mavis gambled, then was too polite
to Sarah's sister. The troupe got right again, but
foreign gentlemen wanted Sarah. He would have allowed
it, but she would not permit it. If she was to get
her living as a whore she might as well stay in her
own country, she said.
    A great swell paid a heavy sum to see her nearly
naked, with boots and stockings on, and in a recumbent
bawdy posture. That she allowed, for the money he
paid was great; but her husband was in the room at the
time. She insisted on that.
    Then a *large* sum was offered for the whole
troupe to perform naked. Some would, some would not—
Sarah would not. Her man should not see her sister
naked, she was determined, and one woman would not
permit her man to be naked. It ended in a row. One
half of the troupe gave private exhibitions naked.
"But," said Sarah, "lots of them don't look so nice
naked as they may think." '

Poor Sarah had discovered, like so many girls, that poverty was a hard-pressing master; and indeed the life of the ballet girl or chorus girl in nineteenth-century Europe was so exhausting, so degrading, that it is a wonder any of them survived to grow old. Some, of course, did not. The introduction of gas-lighting into theatres made fire a great risk; many girls died when the muslin dresses in which they danced and posed caught fire at the footlights, the best known of them being the popular dancer Clara Webster, whose dress caught fire at a performance of Balfe's *The Daughter of St Mark* lit by oil-lamps with naked flames.

At the Royal Academy Exhibition of 1889 a pathetic *genre* painting was exhibited by Claude Calthrop, entitled *The Little Bread Winner*, in

The Police Gazette, **a Victorian journal whose preoccupation with chorus girls was concentrated on their less artistic activities, published this drawing in 1897**

which in an impoverished garret, a mother is showing to her two young sons a little girl of five or six dressed in a fairy costume, her wings at her feet (which are in diminutive ballet shoes), and her wand ready at her hand. This was how a great many dancers started their theatrical careers, for from the 1840s at least groups of children were used in pantomimes and sometimes in other shows, recruited from the poorest homes, and becoming in truth the bread-winners.

An artist going back-stage at the Drury Lane pantomime of 1871 remembered a theatre alive with young children between the ages of seven and thirteen waiting to rehearse their sequence. A small girl would perhaps start as a 'flying fairy', become an extra, then a member of the *corps de ballet*, and finally a *coryphée*. 'The extra,' said Albert Smith, the author of *The Natural History of the Ballet Girl*, published in 1847,

'is still very young and probably undernourished.
Her pay is at present very little—very little
indeed—perhaps a shilling a night: and for this she
has to trot backwards and forwards upon her thin legs,
between her home and the theatre, sometimes four times a
day . . .'

With luck, she might eventually catch the eye of the ballet-master, and be allowed to fetch his beer or peel the potatoes for his dinner, in exchange for being taught a ballet step or two, while 'her leisure time, when she gets any, which is but seldom, is passed in sitting with her feet in a peculiarly agonising pair of stocks, which induce the power of pointing the toes until they form a line with the leg.'

Even when she was engaged for the *corps*, her life was far from enviable; though she then received perhaps fifteen shillings a night—'a perfect fortune'—her existence was hardworking and enclosed enough to be unhealthy:

'The night's work only commences when the night
is far advanced; and the effects of this artificial
existence are usually painfully visible; their cheeks
hollow and pale, even in spite of the daub of vermilion
hastily applied by the dresser; and their limbs nipped
and wasted. . . .'

Mr Smith leaves a vivid picture of the daily grind of the ballet-girl, of life at rehearsal and performance:

'The *coryphées* now arrive, as well as the *corps
de ballet*; the former holding a higher rank and
receiving a higher salary than the latter. They
are pretty, trim-built girls, with sallow faces and
large eyes—the pallor that overspreads their features
resulting from cosmetics and late hours. They work
very hard, and get very little sleep; but they appear

'A Christmas Transformation—Morning—Night'. The Victorian sentimentality of this magazine illustration is pointed, but also accurate

to be very merry amongst themselves for all that.
They are petite in figure, and neatly dress'd in dark
stuff cloaks, or check "polkas" and little black
velvet or drawn bonnets. The *corps de ballet* immediately
prepare to dance; and the others, who will not be
wanted until the *divertissement* in the second act,
run upstairs to the wardrobe to see about their dresses . . .

It is curious to see [the *coryphées*] rehearsing
their *grand pas* in their walking dresses . . . They catch
the notion of any particular step or figure with singular
facility: especially those to whom the honour of a
place in the front rank is assigned. Sometimes, but
very seldom, the stereotypical smile of the evening
breaks out at rehearsal, beaming at the dark void of
the house before them, or even at the stage manager, who
is the nearest approach to the ogres of old that they
can fancy . . .

'About half-past three or four o'clock, the rehearsal concludes; and the ballet-girl, very tired, quits the theatre, to be there again a little after six. All this time she has had no refreshment: and she possibly lives over half-an-hour's walk from the theatre. It may be wet, too, and her thin shoes are not very well calculated to meet the treacherous paths and crossings of the suburbs.'

Back-stage conditions for the ladies of the chorus have always been indifferent: the dressing-rooms, for instance, are always at the top of the theatre—the stars, on the other hand, usually change happily at stage-level. Smith's description of an 1840s dressing-room might serve for today. Five girls shared one room:

'which has two long dressers against its sides, divided into compartments, each containing a common looking-glass and a few mysterious pomatum and rouge-pots, combs, powder-dabblers, scraps of silver-leaves and "logies", [zinc "jewels" made up to look like the real thing], and a wash-hand stand in the middle.

And then the toilet commences, and the dresser has a hard time of it. For the waist of the dress is too short, or the skirts too long, or the white comes below the tarlatan, or the wings won't fit at all to the shoulders, but droop down as if they were going to fall off like those of the Mountain Sylph . . .'

Despite her hard life, the ballet-girl found time to relax, and was often to be seen at the Portland Rooms or at Weipperts—the Hanover Rooms or Willis's—favourite dance-halls where half-guinea charity balls would be held. There she would go, dressed up in what finery she could command, perhaps with an admirer or perhaps hoping to discover one: though as Mr Smith reveals, that perennial dragon the dancer's Mother was often on the scene:

'They have all got Mothers,' he says, somewhat wearily, 'who are the ladies-patronesses of strange bonnets and abnormal dresses. The more rigid ones come to the theatre every night to fetch their daughters home, and are allowed by the stage-doorkeeper to stand inside his lodge, and near the fire in winter. And in no manner will they permit any one else to see their young ladies home, unless he pays them very great attention, or is their proper accepted admirer. And even then he must, to find favour in the eyes of the mother, be somehow or other connected with the profession.'

REGISTERED AT THE G. P. O. AS A NEWSPAPER.

THE MILLION

· EDITED ·
= BY =
GEO. NEWNES.

No. 37, Vol. 2.] FOR THE WEEK ENDING SATURDAY, DECEMBER 3, 1892. [Price One Penny.

A PANTOMIME REHEARSAL.

2 Ballet, Burlesque & Pantomime

The ballet girl, however much she might have had, in the 1840s, a flavour of the chorus girl about her, remained—however tenuously—connected with 'art'. Her sisters who took part in burlesque were much closer to 'the chorus'—though in the end it was a sort of marriage of the two which resulted in the dancing chorus-girl of the 1920s.

It was during the 1840s that burlesque took the London stage: it consisted chiefly of what we would now call 'send-ups' of contemporary theatrical productions—*Aladdin, or the Wonderful Scamp* or *The Corsican Brothers, or The Troublesome Twins* were excuses for comic songs and sketches, often larded with awful puns; and eventually for more or less undressed young ladies, for the ballet with its skimpy costumes was thoroughly parodied—an excuse for presenting girls with even skimpier costumes.

James Robertson Planché was the king of burlesque, also presenting burlettas and extravaganzas, leaning rather towards music than sketches. Many of the latter were presented during the Easter holidays, and so became known as 'Easter pieces'; they were based on fairy tales, often, though they eventually led to revue (originally a French notion). In Planché's *The New Planet! or Harlequin out of Place*, girls were already playing an important part, apparently both as dancers and as statuesque beauties rather like those later to grace the stage of the Gaiety or Daly's. *The Illustrated London News* described how the audience was 'carried through the . . . Egyptian Hall, with its opposition nigger Serenaders, the Haunt of the Wilis, with the different Giselles from the Opera, Drury Lane, the Adelphi, the Princess's, etc . . . and the extravaganza winds up with Harlequin's *tableaux vivants*, by living statues of celebrities, and the enthronization of the new planet.'

At the Haymarket in 1854, John Buckstone, in *A new and original Cosmiographical, Visionary Extravaganza and Dramatic Review*, offered 'Miss Lydia Thompson, Miss L. Morris and the *corps de ballet*' for the delight of his audiences, and in the following year introduced some '*femmes volantes*' into 'a glittering "last scene" ' of another revue.

The girls were beginning to make their mark as objects of admiration —and incidentally it was the same Lydia Thompson who was to take a troupe of 'Visiting British Blondes' to America a few years later, and was largely to provide the impetus for the start of burlesque there— though that was to take a very different direction from British burlesque, becoming in time variety productions, vastly popular entertainments which filled such theatres and halls as the Winter Garden in New York—where Minsky's famous company played—and finally disintegrating, after a degeneration into semi-pornography and strip-tease, in the 1940s.

Planché wrote over 170 entertainments, and many of them introduced ladies in tights (often as solo acts, but sometimes in groups); and at the same time, *opera bouffe* began to be popular. In 1865, *Orpheus in the Haymarket* made use of Offenbach's music, and two years later the first really notable *opera bouffe* production was staged at Covent Garden, where Augustus Harris produced *The Grand Duchess*. *Opera bouffe* had its supply of beautiful girls, and sometimes crossed the lines of decency

'*Over and over again must mothers have blushed . . . at the exhibition of female anatomy to which the "highly respectable" pantomime has introduced children . . . There can be charming ballets without reducing the coryphée almost to nudity.*'

W. Davenport Adams, 1882

The cover of a sheet music selection from Babil and Bijou (see p. 23), written by Dion Boucicault and J. R. Planché, and produced at Covent Garden in 1872, and later at the Alhambra. An elegant corps of gardeners, whose shovels and watering-cans are as elegant as their green baize aprons!

Above: Chorus girls, c. 1893, receive expert instruction in fencing before they appear as 'Musketeers of the Guard'

Below: In The Princess Radiant **at the Haymarket in 1851, the Commander of the Guard appeared in Mrs Bloomer's newfangled garments**

In the Drury Lane pantomime Robinson Crusoe **at the end of the last century, fairy guardsmen showed ample feminine charms**

while indulging in vestigial sword-play. The Fairy King (left) is unimpressed

so that audiences who visited it as an alternative to the more obviously shocking 'naughtiness' of burlesque, were surprised—as by *Vert-Vert* at the St James's in the 1870s, when 'some skanty frocks and an indecent dance' lost Richard Mansell his licence.

Producers were by now thoroughly conscious of the importance of a pretty leg when it came to attracting an audience. Emily Soldene, who in 1871 was producing condensed versions of comic opera in Islington, wrote in her memoirs:

'From the first moment of going into management—
recognising the attractive force of female beauty—I
surrounded myself with the best-looking and best
set-up girls that could possibly be found. I selected
my chorus from the ballet. The result, a minimum of
voice, perhaps, but certainly a maximum of good looks
and grace . . . They felt the music, were full of life,
and, like a blooded horse, were anxious for a start.'

They had not, one is forced to conclude, a very great deal to do. There was usually a *pas seul* for a principal dancer (Kate Vaughan, for instance, who moved freely about the stage in a soft, clinging dress with a full but un-bulky skirt, which was often pleated, and held and displayed to great effect). But the chorus was generally encouraged only to sway gently in time to the music—though in a wonderfully elegant manner, forming contrasting groups and patterns, occasionally with a graceful waltz-kick to enliven the proceedings.

Nevertheless, the ladies of the chorus contributed a very great deal to the success of an evening at the burlesque or the *opera bouffe*—particularly in the display of costumes, which were often very beautiful, and which in the ambitious settings provided, often had a great effect. Planché at his most ambitious evidently provided some impressive scenes—as in *Babil and Bijou*, produced at Covent Garden and subsequently at the Alhambra, in 1872, with the backing of Sir George Sitwell. *The Daily Telegraph* enthused:

'The scene in which Princess Fortinbrasse reviews
her Amazonian troops will no doubt soon become the
talk of the town. Such a glitter of gold, such
burnished armour, such tossing plumes and jewelled
headdresses, such tunics of brown and blue, and black
and scarlet, such lavish wealth, such fringes of
bullion, such lances and swords gleaming in the
limelight, such drummers and bandsmen in Royal
apparel, such comely faces, and such superb specimens
of womanhood, have never surely yet been combined
with such scenes . . .'

If that sounds a little like a pantomime, it is true that the Principal Boy was already on the scene. Charles Dickens wrote to his friend

Forster, in the 1870s, describing a burlesque entitled *The Maid and the Magpie*:

'There is the strangest thing in it that ever I
have seen on the stage—the boy Pippo, by Miss
Walton. While it is astonishingly impudent (must be,
or it couldn't be done at all), it is so stupendously
like a boy, and unlike a woman, that it is perfectly
free from offence. I have never seen such a thing.
She does an imitation of the dancing of the Christy
Minstrels—wonderfully clever—which, in the
audacity of its thorough-going is surprising. A
thing that you cannot imagine a woman doing at all:
and yet the manner, the appearance, the levity, impulse,
and spirits of it are so exactly like a boy that you
cannot think of anything like her sex in association
with it . . .'

The transvestite Principal Boy hero/heroine of traditional English pantomime also took a part in burlesque, as did the boy-girls who formed her court. These were always more for the pleasure of the papas than of the children; girls in tights (particularly during a period when the lower limbs even of pianos were carefully covered) provided an annual exhibition of sexuality which must have been anticipated with equal delight in the nursery and the smoking-room. Many girls looked forward to the annual London pantomimes as an almost unique means of earning a penny or two: Drury Lane, at Christmas-time—where Augustus Harris would sometimes employ as many as 400 extras with work—was a Mecca for the unemployed chorus girl or would-be chorus girl. A comic song of the period ran:

'She only works at Christmas-time,
And at Drury Lane she's found.
She earns enough in the pantomime
To keep her the whole year round.'

It might be thought that the chorus girl in pantomime, if as vulgar as her sister in burlesque, missed out on any opportunities for elegance. Not so. Augustus Harris in particular produced pantomimes of great taste and opulence. *Dick Whittington*, at Drury Lane in 1895 (with the famous Dan Leno and Herbert Campbell as comedians) had as its centrepiece The Feast of Lanterns, given in honour of the Princess Ni-Si-Pi-See's marriage. *The Theatre* reported:

'So far as beauty of colouring, richness of
dressing, and variety of effects are concerned, the
spectacle, it may safely be affirmed, has never
been surpassed. Down two broad staircases, a glittering
host of mandarins, standard-bearers, pages, attendants,

Costume designs for three productions at George Edwardes' Gaiety Theatre: Above: 'An Officer' in Ruy Blas, or the Blasé Roué **(1889); Right: original designs by Alfred Thompson for** Hawaya **and** Monte Cristo Junior **(1886)**

guests, dancing-girls, and officials descends
until the stage becomes one mass of glowing hues.
Especially noticeable is one party of guests clad in
armour of the willow-plate pattern. Suddenly,
wreaths, floral ornaments, and candelabra are
illuminated by the electric light with a magical
result, from which the dazzled eye of the beholder
is almost fain to turn away for relief.'

But the blaze of electric light did not only reveal the beauties of the
chorus girls in hooped skirts or even ballet *tutus*. It also illuminated the
sturdy thighs—well, er, 'lower limbs'—of the Principal Boy and of 'his'
companions, equally obviously feminine, and indulging in most
un-ladylike horse-play in the cut-out forests of fairyland. And, worse
still, the antics of the female 'Dames', played by often rather un-
prepossessing elderly men.

The 'honest vulgarity' of pantomime (that is how the Edwardian
puritan pantomime enthusiast excused it) did not impress some critics,
who genuinely saw in the flashing legs of the girls (even of the 'girl'
girls in their brief dresses) a danger to morals quite as keen as anything
which can be discerned on today's television.

In 1882, W. Davenport Adams launched a severe attack on the 'corrupting' influence of pantomime, in his column in *The Theatre*. He mainly complained of the vulgarity of the music-hall comedians in the leading roles—who brought with them their 'songs, which when offensive in their wording are sometimes made doubly dangerous by their tunefulness'; but he also suggested that the producers seemed to be satisfying the instincts not of the children brought to the pantomime in such numbers by their fathers and mothers, but of the Victorian papas. There were, in pantomime, displays of 'the feminine form' which were positively lubricious:

'It must surely be conceded,' suggested Mr Adams,
'that the rows of infinitesimally clothed damsels who
crowd the pantomime stage are not the sort of spectacle
to which it is judicious to introduce "the young
idea", especially when it is at the age at which
curiosity concerning the forbidden is beginning to

At a Drury Lane pantomime (right) the gentlemen apparently so attentive to their children were not unmoved by the charms of the ladies of the chorus. Far Right: Walter Sickert, chronicler of the theatre and music-hall, painted the gallery, whence came more outspoken and rumbustious cries of approval when the girls showed a leg

display itself . . . Over and over again must mothers have blushed (if they were able to do so) at the exhibition of female anatomy to which the "highly respectable" pantomime has introduced children . . . There can be charming ballets without reducing the *coryphée* almost to nudity. Processions can be so costumed as to be eminently picturesque without impropriety.'

Mr Adams was not alone in his protests; but neither was he successful. Critics have always argued that fairy stories are for children; managers have always realised that it is father who pays for the theatre seat, and that it is advisable that he shall not be entirely bored. The whole notion of the girl-boy has sexual connotations that would no doubt shock some of those very fathers; but it is a tradition so old that its significance is often missed.

3 **Paris**

The serious English theatre has always been a little insular; but foreign influences on the chorus certainly cannot be discounted, especially in the last years of the last century; the influence, for instance, of Paris.

In 1845 or so, the polka, then the *polka-piquée*, in which the dancers kicked up their legs as high as possible, was very popular in the French capital—except with the moralists, who not only objected to the girls showing their frothy knickers, but more sturdily objected to the fact that the dance appeared to create even more interest from the gentlemen in the audience when the ladies wore no knickers at all, which was quite often the case.

The *polka-piquée* became extremely popular in dance-halls frequented by prostitutes. The Vicomte de Saint-Laurent (in his *Observations on Modern Dancing*) pointed out that 'for many, the polka would seem to be but the prelude to whoring, for they visit their mistresses immediately after the ball. And even those who do not go so far are stimulated by the intimate rhythmic bodily contacts of the dance into sexual fantasies involving their partners . . .'

Logically, performers soon modified the *polka* (always danced with a partner) into a dance suitable for performance on-stage by a soloist, or, more often, a group or 'chorus'. From a sort of cross between the *polka-piquée* and the *quadrille naturaliste* came the *Robert Macaire*, then the *chahut*, and finally the can-can, which soon (as Théophile Gautier put it) 'captured the imagination and delight of truly decent people—despite the activity of the police.'

The can-can, danced by a soloist or a chorus, was an even less artistic variant of the *polka-piquée*, in which the whole intention was to display the legs in a series of leaps and kicks and 'splits'—again, often without knickers: the *can-can sans culottes* was a dance which originally owed much more to the brothel ante-room than to the stage, and its intention was outright titillation, prostitutes being in attendance to satisfy the itches aroused in the customer (much as prostitutes in twentieth century cities often rent rooms as close as possible to the exits of strip-clubs). It was perhaps a dance more notorious than evident, though there is no doubt that it *was* performed, and that stories of its aphrodisiac delights came back to convince potential tourists of the advantages of Paris.

(The can-can only ever reached England in a modified and polite form; though it was considered daring enough when it first reached London and the stage of the Princess's Theatre, during a performance of *The Huguenot Captain* in 1866. At Christmas 1867 it was a special feature of W. S. Gilbert's pantomime *Cock Robin*; and later, in a Gaiety burlesque, *Ali Baba*, a troupe appeared as The Dancing Quakers and performed a can-can, which led to a public apology when the Society of Friends protested.)

Only the paintings and drawings of the period gave a real impression of the gaiety and excitement of the can-can. The few early photographs which exist have only the strain and tension evoked by the girls having to adopt a 'can-can pose' and hold it—for the photographs were taken before the camera's shutter-speed was fast enough to be able to catch them in the real bouncing bonhomie of the dance.

'Pretty heads, pretty shoulders, pretty legs . . . as much as one could wish for. More than one could wish for !'

Daniel Auber, 1847

The can-can, a decidedly 'naughty' French dance, was an excuse for high kicks and the flashing of underwear. This young lady, in a very early photograph (c. 1890) is decorous but attractive, and a strong dancer – for her raised leg would have been held in position for several seconds at least, to be caught by the camera

At what might seem the other end of the spectrum, the ballet girls of the Opéra, though not indulging in bottomless *polka-piquée*, were also ancestresses of the chorus girl in the sense that they were on display before the eyes of men less interested in culture than in the swell of a bosom or the length of a leg.

Charles Yriarte described in the 1860s the kind of entertainment the Opéra provided:

'The man of fashion at the Opéra, with his box or
his stall, his favourite dancer, his opera-glass, and
his right of entry back-stage, has a horror of anything
which remains on the bills for a long time, of anything
artistic, which must be listened to, respected, or
requires an effort to be understood. The man of fashion . . .
has little use for the sublime strophes of the great
Gluck; he wants the brisk and lively melodies of M. Auber,
the adorable flutterings of Mlle Fioretti or Mlle Fonte . . .

'I wager that eight out of every ten *abonnés* prefer
Pierre de Médicis to the fourth act of *Les Huguenots*,
and *Néméa* to *Guillaume Tell*. And why? Simply because
Louise Fiocre shows her limbs in *Pierre*, and her younger
sister Eugénie shows much more than that in *Néméa* . . .'

It was during the 1860s and 1870s at the Paris Opéra that many of the legends of back-stage immorality arose, which have plagued the lives of chorus girls ever since. It was certainly true that it was then the ambition of every right-thinking man of fashion to be the 'protector' of an Opéra girl—and it was well-known that any man who was in such a position must be one of a select minority with the right of entry into the Foyer de la Danse.

The Foyer, just behind the stage at the Opéra, was not outwardly opulent or gracious: it had originally been designed for rehearsals, and ostensibly that was still its purpose. Its floor sloped, with the same slope as the stage, down towards a large mirror—so that the rehearsing dancers could see themselves as the audience would see them—, and a *barre* ran around the other three sides.

But after the Revolution of 1830, the Foyer had attained a new notoriety, for then a few of the most distinguished *abonnés* had been allowed to go back-stage during performances, and the Foyer had become the place where they could walk or lounge, watching the dancers as they moved to and from the stage to their dressing-rooms. Some of those girls entered, through the Foyer and its fashionable attendants, into the kind of life they dreamed about. Léo Lespès, in 1864, pointed out that

'since the Restoration Swiss village girls, peasants
from the Abruzzi, and flower-girls from the Marche des
Innocents have been seen with 6,000 francs glittering
at the tips of their ears and emerald rings more numerous
than those worn on her fingers by the beauty imprisoned
in the depths of the sea.'

Above: An early stereoscopic photograph of girls, perhaps in the green-room where they would receive visitors

Right: At the turn of the century, two girls in an early action photograph making up in forthright vivacity and charm what they may lack as beauties: decorous lace underneath suggests a gentility certainly not of the Paris dance-halls!

Most of the men who haunted the Foyer were members of the famous and exclusive Jockey Club (which regularly established itself in seven of the proscenium boxes and one large *baignoire* at the Opéra, and regarded the theatre 'as a sort of fief'). The President of the Club, the Vicomte Paul Daru, is described as striding about the Foyer like a Sultan in a Seraglio, bowing to someone here, smiling at someone there, apparently familiar even with the smallest and least distinguished *rat* or *marcheuse*. And most of the really fashionable men of the city managed by hook or by crook to gain admission: Prosper Merimée, Théophile Gautier, Meyerbeer, Adam and Auber—who, with a satisfied sigh, once looked about him and remarked: 'Pretty heads, pretty shoulders, pretty legs . . . as much as one could wish for. More than one could wish for!'

Right and below: Backstage at the Paris Opera: top-hatted gentlemen flirt with the girls while the chorus-men and scene-shifters go about their business. Below right: A drawing from La Vie Parisienne suggests girls of a more oncoming disposition

The girls received the attentions of these fashionable admirers with great *sang-froid*—again adding to the cachet of naughtiness which was to attach itself to their more respectable sisters at other theatres. They smiled and chattered and preened, and sooner or later came to arrangements and accommodations with the gentlemen, more or less rewarding according to their business-sense. Sometimes, their mothers bargained for them. Comte Albert de Maugny, familiar with the Foyer, wrote:

'Epic scenes took place [at the stage-door]. I
have seen damsels departing triumphantly on an admirer's
arm after a good quarter of an hour's parlay with *maman*.
I have seen damsels disappear surreptitiously behind their
duenna's back, leaving her prey to an epileptic agitation;
and others carrying on brazenly beneath their very nose
and receiving a volley of blows that would have frightened
a street-porter.'

Mothers were not allowed in the Foyer, but guarded its exit with great verve; and sometimes turned manager in a sense that would outrage our sensibilities. Ludovic Halévy, turning up one day at the home of a girl with whom he had 'an arrangement', was greeted by her mother in a state of violent agitation:

'Ah, *monsieur*, we cannot receive you today!' she
cried breathlessly; 'If only you knew! We have a king
in there—a king!'

And indeed she may not have been lying, for the Opéra girls had become famous as courtesans. While a few doubtless remained respectable, most behaved as though they were members of the world's

MURGA

STEBBING
PARIS

WALERY
PARIS

most exclusive brothel, and some commanded enormous fees. The King of Piedmont, visiting Napoleon III, was outraged when he learned that the girl he most admired in the *corps de ballet* demanded an 'acknowledgement' of 50 louis—and if Napoleon had not graciously commanded the girl to 'charge it to my account', he might have left Paris unsatisfied.

A few of the ballet girls—Pauline Mercier, Eline Volter, Amélie Hairivau (beautiful, tall and slender, with hips 'worthy of an Andalusian' and very small feet, we are mouth-wateringly informed)—were as famous as any great courtesans. Some of them behaved outrageously, like Clara Pilvois, who once did a wild can-can in the Foyer during a rehearsal, and commonly wore her diamonds to class!

Even the balletomanes who were really interested in the dance itself, as an art form, had an eye for beauty which was a great deal more lubricious than any ballet-critic's could today afford to be—at least in print. In one notice published in 1837, Théophile Gautier, the best of the early ballet critics, wrote:

'Mlle Fanny Elssler is tall, supple, and well-
formed; she has delicate wrists and slim ankles; her
legs, elegant and well-formed, recall the slender but
muscular legs of Diana, the virgin huntress; the knee-
caps are well-defined, stand out in relief, and make the
whole knee beyond reproach; her legs differ considerably
from the usual dancers' legs, whose bodies seem to have
run into their stockings and settled there; they are not the
calves of a parish beadle or of a jack of clubs which
arouse the enthusiasm of the old roués in the stalls and
make them continuously polish the lenses of their opera-
glasses, but two beautiful legs like those of an antique
statue, worthy of being studied with care . . .
    Her bosom is full, a rarity among dancers, where
the twin hills and mountains of snow—so praised by students
and minor poets—appear totally unknown!'

While the management of the Opéra was sufficiently conscious of its need for the support of the fashionable to allow goings-on in the Foyer which would certainly not be encouraged at any theatre in the world today, there was strict discipline to safeguard the smooth running of the ballets themselves, whatever the morals of the performers.

A list of penalties was published, which would be imposed on

'every artiste of the *corps de ballet* who creates a disturbance
during the performance by talking or laughing in the
theatre, distracting the attention of persons on the stage,
or applauding or showing disapproval in any manner
whatsoever; who interferes with the stage management by
causing an obstruction in the wings, arriving before the
call, or talking too loudly; who interferes with the
scene-shifting; who comes into view of the audience;

Three stunning ladies from the Paris of the turn of the century: the costumes were not as daring as they seem—body-stockings were worn, though the lines at neck and shoulders were 'touched out' in the photographs, and masked by make-up in performance. The dark beauty in the ample tulle bikini (bottom) has a figure which confirms the fashion for slim waists and ample hips

Degas delighted in the ballet girls of the opera, painting and drawing them clothed and unclothed: the paintings often reveal the slender technique the girls possessed as dancers

who makes a noise behind the curtain; in short, who shows lack in any way whatsoever of consideration towards others, of the respect owed to the public, of decency, and of discipline at performance or rehearsal.'

For first offences, dancers were suspended from certain performances; repetitions would lead to a loss of salary, to fines and redoubled fines; and finally 'any artist who is fined three times in the same month incurs . . . termination of engagement and expulsion from the theatre.'

Though members of the Jockey Club were perhaps not too concerned with what the ballet girl actually *did* (on-stage, at least) Gautier and other critics have at least left a description of the choreography of the period, which doubtless at its best seemed exquisite. Whether it would seem so today, is a little doubtful, and we might think, if we could see them, that the ballet-girls of the early Romantic Ballet acted more like ambitious chorus girls than anything else. Even their pyrotechnics were limited: there were no strongly blocked ballet-shoes, so the dancer could not perform at any length on full pointe, only occasionally rising onto the tips of her toes in a simple *relevé*.

What the stage of the Opéra offered, above all, was a display of delicacy and grace and beauty, sometimes delightfully light and airy, sometimes surprisingly statuesque. The attentions of the Jockey Club, the demand for 'just' beauty, may have been in part responsible for the downward slide of what ballet technique there was. The candid back-stage drawings of Degas show a galaxy of bent knees, forced and 'sickled' feet, arched backs and uncontrolled hips. The ballet girl became in the end almost indistinguishable from the chorus girl with whom we are preoccupied; later, of course, with Diaghilev and the Russian Ballet, she was to make her brilliant come-back, and to go on to triumphs which lift her way beyond our scope.

But in the late 1800s, while she was still extending a shapely leg and a neat ankle from the stage of the Opéra in the direction of the Vicomte Daru and his friends, she was in spirit and sometimes in fact much closer to her sisters performing elsewhere in the city, where regulations may have been less enforceable, and the girls even less inhibited and discreet.

At various dance-halls in the city, there were 'floor shows' performed by small groups of girls—the most famous quartet appearing regularly at the Elysée-Montmartre, where Henri Toulouse-Lautrec watched them perform the *quadrille naturaliste*, a fairly simple 'dance' which had evolved from the now rather dated can-can. It consisted of a series of high-kicks: the women kicked over the heads of their partners (sometimes professional, sometimes visitors to the halls), then grasped an ankle high above their heads, dancing on the other foot.

The pleasure of the dance was of course in the display of shapely legs in black silk stockings, of lace petticoats, and perhaps a glimpse of bare thigh below the black silk knickers—a pleasure for the man not sufficiently adventurous to visit the more bawdy pleasure-houses. From the four girls who appeared at the Elysée-Montmartre in 1886, one star emerged: Louise Weber, known as La Goulue.

The dancers were carefully watched for any undue indecency: any dancers who failed to wear the prescribed black knickers (La Goulue's had a red heart embroidered on the seat!) were supposed to be warned off the floor; but at private nights, 'le Père-la-Pudeur', as the censor was called, was excluded, and baskets of fig-leaves were carried around and distributed to the dancers at midnight—by which time they were often needed.

The world-famous Moulin Rouge opened in the autumn of 1889 at the corner of the Place Blanche and the Rue Lepec, as a dance hall with 'entertainments'. These consisted at first of troupes of high-kicking dancers who displayed their enthusiasm and their legs in a routine, and then circulated among the audience, where the exchange of favours and of money was not unknown.

In the gardens, where there were little individual enclosures, and on the minute dance-floor, the *quadrille naturaliste* was performed, to the considerable danger of those who used the hall as much for promenading or embracing as for dancing, the high kicks occasionally injuring ladies and gentlemen who happened to be passing.

La Goulue and Valentin at the Moulin Rouge, as seen by Toulouse-Lautrec

Charles Zidler, the proprietor, was obviously a man of great skill: soon, he had tempted La Goulue away from the Elysée-Montmartre, together with her great partner Valentin, and other stars or future stars; the ladies of what passed for 'the chorus' followed their betters, and there was much competition for the right to appear at the Moulin Rouge, where for some time the greatest attraction was Le Pétomane, that large gentleman who could execute almost any tune requested of him in a series of musical farts.

It is through the posters and sketches of Lautrec that we know this period of the dance-halls of Paris so well; and because he concentrated on the stars—La Goulue and Valentin, later Jane Avril and Yvette Guilbert, Cissie Loftus and May Belfort and Chocolat and the rest—one tends to forget the girls who formed the background to their acts. But they were not, anyway, yet an organised chorus: they were still individuals, even if they all performed the same, rather stereotyped dance steps.

It was at one particular theatre that, for the English or German or American tourist of the first half of the present century, the naughtiest, most titillating, sexiest show in the world was to be found; and though its stars always attracted considerable attention, it was the 'girls' who brought in the crowds.

The Folies Bergère opened on 1 May, 1869. In the eighteenth century, a piece of parkland where bushes provided adequate cover for alfresco love-making was known as a *folie*, and a little later *folies* were places of public entertainment where there was drinking and a certain amount of light entertainment conducive to a romantic evening. The new theatre was at first to be called the Folies Trévise; but the Duc de Trévise did not take kindly to the idea. Locals were already calling it 'The Elastic Mattress' (though only because of a mattress-shop which had once been on the site). Finally, it was called the Folies Bergère, after a M. Bergier—a master-dyer who had worked for years on the site.

It seemed a good time to open a theatre: Louis-Napoleon's Second Empire was at its brilliant apogee, and the founders of the theatre foresaw a great financial success. Then, on 1 September, 1870, came the defeat at Sedan. The Chamber of Deputies was invaded; the Republic proclaimed. Within one *année terrible*, as Victor Hugo called it, the Commune had risen and fallen, the centre of Paris was in ruins, and 20,000 Parisiens had been slaughtered by their fellows.

So apart from a few weeks of gaiety, the Folies Bergère's first use was as a political meeting-place, a centre for political rallies, often addressed by Rochefort and Michelet, two of the finest orators of the period. But when peace came, it reverted to its original purpose, and its manager, Léon Sari, organised entertainments of a circus sort—a woman with two heads, a spectacular juggler, 'a prodigious magician who swallows live snakes, tears open his stomach and pulls out rosaries and pears which he presents to the ladies.'

Sari also provided dancing-girls, of course—a *corps* which provided for the ordinary middle-class man a spectacle halfway between the parade of ballet-girls presented for the aristocracy at the Opéra, and the openly outrageous ladies of the dancing-halls.

At the back of the Folies was a *promenoir*—an open space behind the

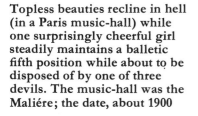

Topless beauties recline in hell (in a Paris music-hall) while one surprisingly cheerful girl steadily maintains a balletic fifth position while about to be disposed of by one of three devils. The music-hall was the Maliére; the date, about 1900

stalls where one could stroll with a drink among a number of ladies whose virtue was more apparent than real (and not very apparent, at that). It was to remain a feature of the Folies for many years, and was always to arouse the passions of reformers: 'the most notorious "ladies" of the district frequent it assiduously and it enjoys thereby the questionable privilege of attracting the hordes of foreigners sojourning in the capital,' wrote one journalist. Many of the foreigners would no doubt have been familiar with the Empire, Leicester Square, where promenading ladies were an equally attractive feature of the evening's entertainment.

Sari, for one reason or another, actually tried at one period to reform his theatre, removing not only the ladies of the *promenoir* but the ladies of the chorus too, replacing them with a choir which sang classical music under the batons of Gounod, Massenet and Delibes. The public did not respond to the change in the way he had hoped, and almost bankrupt he was bought out by a rich patroness for the brothers Émile and Vincent Isola, two conjurers. They turned the Folies into a great variety theatre, with the best circus turns in Europe performing there.

It was their successors, M. and Mme. Lallemand, who presented the theatre's first revue—*Place au Jeune*, which opened in November 1886. They also constructed a dance-floor in the garden at the back of the theatre, and staffed the bars with beautiful barmaids whose attention to the convenience of the patrons was notably effective (Manet immortalised one of them in a famous painting). Inside the theatre, a parade of some of the most beautiful cocottes of the period aroused the senses; the proprietors' nephew, Edouard Marchand, organised the first real chorus of 'girls'—as yet more or less fully, if beautifully, clad.

It was a crusader against vice and exhibitionism who was responsible for the transformation of the Folies into ostensibly the sexiest theatre in Europe. The story started in the Place Blanche on the evening of the Four Arts Ball of 1893, when the art students of Paris met at the Moulin Rouge for a night of traditional extravagance. At midnight, a covey of some of the artists' models became involved in an argument as to who had the most beautiful legs in the city. A parade of legs led soon enough to a parade in which other areas of the body were presented for the judgement of Paris; and a lady who deserves a certain amount of celebration—one Mona—eventually threw off all her clothes and invited the students to elect her undisputed queen of the models. The evening ended cheerfully.

Next morning, however, Senator Beranger, a gentleman who habitually busied himself with the morals of the city, and had formed a League of Decency whose main preoccupation had so far been to stop dogs urinating in the street (not on the grounds of sanitation, but on the grounds that this was an example of indecent exposure) set to work to trace those responsible for the display at the Moulin Rouge the night before. Several weeks later, Mona and two or three of her admirers were brought before a Paris court. The magistrates leniently fined them a mere 100 francs each. The Latin Quarter, however, was not amused.

Hearing that effigies of himself (labelled *The Father of Decency*) were

Overleaf: A double-page from a programme of the Folies Bergère in the 1920s, splendidly illustrating the slightly comic air of nudity plus high fashion. The ropes of pearls, fashionable hats, are unmistakably amusing in this context; but also unmistakably titillating—the whole secret of the Folies. In 3 pictures, fans are carefully used to hide—not nudity, but the fact that the girls are not nude!

LES COQUETTES dans *LES MIROIRS INDISCRETS*

En haut : CLAY   *En bas :* SYLVETTE   *En haut :* AVELINE   *En bas :* DELIGNY

LES COQUETTES dans *LES MIROIRS INDISCRETS*

En haut : DELIGNY   *En bas :* AVELINE   *En haut :* AVELINE   *En bas :* Ginette GUY

hanging from lamp-posts on the Boulevard St Michel, Senator Beranger summoned the police; and in the fracas an innocent young man quietly drinking *pernod* at a pavement café, was killed. As a result of the ensuing riots, the Chief of Police was dismissed, and the students (of art and of anything else) decided that it was their inalienable right to enjoy the sight of a naked woman if they wanted to.

Well and good, one might think; but the law, of course, was not on their side. How were they to circumvent the attitude of the Senator and his friends? A combination of enthusiasm and cupidity made it possible. Le Divan Fayouau, a little theatre in the Rue des Martyrs, had a manager who devised an entertainment entitled *Le Coucher d'Yvette*. In it, Yvette, a personable young lady not entirely unknown to members of her audience, prepared for bed in what can only be called the first public strip-tease. She never appeared on-stage naked, but imagination being the active force it is, her act was sufficiently lubricious to be quite as effective as if she had.

Her show had much the same effect as the repeal of stage censorship in England 75 years later. *Le Coucher d'Yvette* was followed by *Le Bain de Maid*, *Liane chez Médicin*, and *Suzanne et la Grande Chaleur*—or *Suzy in a Heatwave*, which must have borne a startling resemblance to the strip-films of the 1960s, in which a bored-looking young lady murmuring, 'It's so *hot!*' removed all but her rings.

At the Folies there were less openly daring versions of these mimes; the chorus remained more or less clothed. It was only gradually that more and more areas of 'les girls' became available for public viewing. During the First World War, the breasts of the girls at the Folies became some sort of symbol of what a great number of troops briefly on leave from the agony of the front line thought they were fighting for. There are few descriptions available of the shows of that period, though we are told that Italy's entry into the war was greeted by a parade of 'twenty magnificent girls, dressed in Italian military uniforms, each with one fair breast exposed.'

It was Paul Derval, Director of the Folies Bergère for most of the first half of this century, who presided over its transformation from a more or less commonplace revue theatre into its famous self. With the end of the first war, came the completely (or more or less completely) nude show-girl of the Folies, though in November 1910 a completely nude woman had appeared at the Casino de Paris, in a revue called *Paris qui Danse*. It was soon discovered that while individual stars might come and go to more or less acclaim, the nudes alone, together with the magnificently gowned *mannequins habillées*, were capable of bringing in the crowds. Derval never hesitated to take advantage of the fact. Conscious that the time was right, he introduced the first nude into one of his early post-war revues, without any previous announcement.

She was (he wrote in his memoirs) 'an adorable little blonde, exquisitely made and curly as a lamb. The day she appeared on the stage for the first time, a mesmerised hush fell over the house, followed by an immense sigh of admiration.' She sat quite still on a bank of flowers mounted on wheels, and was pulled across the stage carrying a jewelled bow and arrows, as the goddess of love. She was a non-dancing show-girl, as most nudes were until comparatively recently. 'Les Girls' were professional dancers, who very rarely indeed were called upon to show more than a thigh here and a breast there. Most of them came from England, and certainly those trained by the formidable Tiller organisation were not going to take part in any unnecessary exposure!

The difference between show girl and chorus girl was at first well defined: the chorus girl danced, and sometimes (rather shakily) sang; the show girl—well, showed. But the caution of the earlier revues, in which the nudes occasionally might sway to the music, or move carefully two or three steps across the stage, gradually gave way to a more adventurous period during which apart from the sixteen or twenty show-girls, there would also be sixteen nudes, two of whom would be professional dancers. There would be opportunities for nudes or semi-nudes to take part in genuine dance routines, which were the ancestors of the nude 'ballets' of *Oh, Calcutta!* or *The Dirtiest Show in Town*, in which (in London in the 1970s) a large cast appeared completely naked.

M. Derval's attention to the morality of his girls, while never perhaps as strict as that of the Tillers in the early years of the century, was necessarily careful; he had to recruit many of his dancers from the dancing schools of France and England, and the chances of getting really accomplished girls would have been much less if the Folies had been known as a thoroughly disreputable theatre.

The spectacular revues of the 1920s and 1930s at the Folies wore down the division between chorus girls and show girls to a point at which discrimination was less possible: the entire company often took part in a particular tableau. One of the most famous of Derval's revues was *Chœurs en Folie*, which Figaro described as 'an evocation of the Napoleonic period from the Consulship to the Empire, the Directoire fashions on show only proving that *plus ça change, plus c'est la meme chose.*' There was a midnight fête at the Tivoli Gardens; a *mongolfiére*, or hot-air balloon; a Roman chariot-race; 'a gleaming show-case in which young women in tasteful *déshabillé* represented rings, bracelets, earrings, pendants and clasps,' and 'a Tarasque monster, with terrible eyes and wide-open mouth, belching smoke, all hundred feet of which suddenly dissolved into a graceful, well-trained group of dancers,' and a final number set in Egypt, with a swimming pool in which young ladies demonstrated that the *cache-sexe* was no less aphrodisiac than the one-piece bathing costume. One surviving photograph suggests that there was also a Spanish scene in which 'les Girls' appeared clad only in admittedly very capacious *mantillas*.

Swimming pools, providing an excellent excuse for various degrees of undress, as well as a natural setting for languorous poses, appeared in a number of Paris revues between the wars: at the end of *En douce*, at the Casino de Paris in 1923, the entire cast dived into a glass tank containing twenty thousand gallons of water!

By the 1950s, show-girls and nude dancers at the Folies seem to the interested observer to have become almost interchangeable: the authors recall a performance of an extract from *Swan Lake* in which to say the least the feathers in the dancers' costumes were sparingly distributed. By that time, too, the male dancers were no longer wearing the tights which were traditional at the theatre for some years, but were content with the briefest *cache-sexe*, often flesh-coloured. (Derval, incidentally, used to say that he was 'often' asked to present male nudes at the Folies, but never said from whom the request so regularly came, nor why he refused it.)

When one talks of the famous nudes of the Folies Bergère, one must remember that in fact they were never really nude: a small triangle of fabric was always worn, fixed by spirit gum. Originally, small patches of material were similarly, and no doubt uncomfortably, fixed over the girls' nipples (the story of the poor girl who was allergic to spirit gum, and whose part was always carefully choreographed so that she spent the entire evening facing back-stage, is something of a legend).

The total nudity of the stage shows and films of the 1970s has given the Folies now a somewhat old-fashioned air; perhaps it was a prophetic foresight which prompted one of Derval's young ladies actually to threaten to sue him in the French courts for not permitting her to fulfil her contract, in which she had promised to appear 'toute nue'.

The Folies always remembered that it was in the sex business. Prostitutes had been using the *promenoir* since the turn of the century. The story is that a kindly door-keeper let some of them in, one very cold winter evening, and that within a few months they had so invaded the theatre that the manager had no option other than to regularise the position by issuing the prettiest and best-dressed ones with identity cards which admitted them to certain performances. This at least ensured that the audience was not put out by the appearance of the sleazier ladies of the town, and that there were no unseemly fights over prospective customers.

For a quarter of a century, the system worked well. Many of the male clients, not unaffected by the beautiful girls on the stage, vanished into the night with the lady of their choice, invited by the merest wink or turn of the head (anything more suggestive was frowned upon by the management). It was generally known that in the *promenoir* were to be found the prettiest, most select prostitutes in the city; no doubt this did nothing to keep custom away, and even the ladies in the audience—and there has always been a high proportion of women there—seemed not too outraged. The ladies of Paris always had a sensible attitude to the Folies: if they did not wish to be offended by nudity or prostitution, they simply kept away.

M. Derval, however, decided, between the wars, that the tradition must be changed. It took him some time. Girls turned away from the *promenoir* would reappear, neatly dressed in country clothes, to buy the less expensive seats, which entitled them to walk in the *promenoir* if they wished. But gradually the theatre was 'cleaned up,' and its only crime against morality since then has been to arouse the passions without offering the means to satisfy them.

Unsurprisingly, the Folies Bergère company was tempted to tour; but while invitations to Stockholm, London, Milan, Zurich, Buenos

Left: The Hoffman Girls wait back-stage at the Moulin Rouge in Paris (1924). As the young lady in the foreground demonstrates, their talents were not purely balletic

Below: Joyful anticipation from the only man on-stage at the Casino de Paris in 1945: but the atmosphere is much that of the first nude shows of the century

Aires were readily accepted, it was realised from the first that there was little chance, between the wars, of the show appearing in its original French form. When the Folies came to London, for instance, the utmost degree of nudity allowed on-stage was the presentation of *tableaux vivants* at the Windmill theatre; any girl who happened, even inadvertently, to move while naked on a stage, placed the management in danger of prosecution. The appearance of nude dancers would have given the authorities a collective coronary.

So the Folies had to depend on its costumes for effect—and fortunately, Derval had always stressed the importance of a well-dressed, as well as a well-undressed, show. Many fine designers had given their attention to, say, the bottom half of a magnificent crinoline for a court scene in which the modern equivalent of Marie Antoinette's diamonds had to provide a sufficient decoration from the waist up.

M. Derval found that in most places visited by the company between the wars and for twenty years afterwards, the girls breasts had to be covered. So the Folies travelled with a set of little stars carefully tailored for the breast of each show girl or dancer. Every night, a star one size smaller than that of the previous night would be fixed by spirit gum. After fifteen weeks in Buenos Aires, the stars would be no notable impediment to the visual pleasure of the keenest connoisseur in the audience, and this method also helped to keep the show packed until the end of the longest run.

The emphasis at the Folies during the past twenty years has been rather different from that at other Paris theatres: for one thing, whereas most theatres have their *mannequins nues*, the Folies also has its *mannequins habillées*, whose job has been to show off the magnificent costumes especially designed for the revues, and made in the *ateliers* in the theatre itself. The splendour .of sets and costumes for many of the post-war Folies shows has been memorable indeed; as, it seems, has been the constancy and friendliness of the audience, which has gone to that theatre as to a kind of national or international monument.

The Folies has encouraged, in the oddest but most definite way, a 'family' atmosphere, with a certain degree of brash audience participation, in which the girls lure men onto the stage, where they are garbed in *tutus* or other more or less embarrassing costumes; and by careful use of lighting in the auditorium as well as on-stage, and bringing the girls out into the middle of the audience; people have been involved with the shows in a most enjoyable way.

As is usually the case with the chorus, the job had more outward glamour than material reward. 'The Folies', said one ex-mannequin decidedly, 'must have been the least well-paying famous theatre in the world.' In 1958, she was receiving £12 a week, forced to eat 'on tick' at any restaurant she could find, or to face the somewhat revolting cooking of the *concierge* whose other job was to keep over-zealous admirers out of the theatre.

The French girls working at the Folies often had boy-friends who were supporting them, or were even using the job quite frankly as a marriage-marketplace. Then, they often lived at home, and so more

A Folies Bergère scene in the 1930s (the period placed not so much by the topless girls in the cage, as by the cartooned, monocled men in pasteboard behind it)

cheaply than the English girls who were a feature of the show. (Nowadays, British Actors Equity contract stipulates that any foreign management must pay 'not less than the equivalent of £5 clear over and above the cost of board and lodging.' Even this is not particularly generous, but would have seemed heaven in the Paris of the 1950s).

The Folies Bergère depended to a great extent on its girls, even when Chevalier or Mistinguett were appearing there; the Paris music-hall never placed so much emphasis on groups of dancers or mannequins—though there were some exceptions in the Paris of the 1920s and 1930s, when lines of girls appeared as a support to the stars whose acts really made music-hall the great attraction it was. During the First World War, the extraordinary Damia, at her own theatre, the Concert-Damia, was drawing great crowds to an act which was the epitome of sensuality; elsewhere, Yvonne George and Fréhel had their acts, and the Folies-Marigny was paying Gaby Deslys 200,000 francs to appear in a jazz revue, for jazz was the new craze.

Information about the supporting company is sparse, as, often enough, was the company itself. The stars held the shows together, and the girls who 'filled in' while an impatient audience waited for Deslys or Régine Flory or Jenny Golder were given scant attention by audiences or critics.

But there were certain troupes of girls, not strictly of the chorus, whose acts are still remembered: the Hoffman Girls, for instance, dimly related to a line of high-kickers, but whose speciality was the elasticity and dextrousness of their movements: sixteen or eighteen of them, in tights and leotards, had devised a skilful and fast routine which derived from the films: in one number, 'eighteen girls in white-diamond-studded sweaters, hung by their wrists and teeth from long white cords over the audience's heads . . .'

But in general, the music-hall girls of the period played a much inferior rôle to that of the girls at the Folies. The Blackbirds, then the *Revue Nègre*, caused something of a sensation in a Paris to which Josephine Baker, and such other black artistes as the magnificent Feral Benga, were still novelties; but ordinarily, as Maurice Chevalier somewhat whimsically put it, 'the nude show girl quietly took possession only of the Folies Bergère stage, thus dispensing, by her own unrivalled and perennial appeal, with the need for highly-paid celebrities.' The music-halls did not follow where Derval led. In the photographs of the music-hall revues of the 1930s, it is always the star who is centre-stage—Cecile Sorel at the Casino de Paris, stretching out her arms as wide as her vast crinoline, while the girls behind her in less opulent costumes show no more of themselves than a polite lady at a fashionable evening party; and probably less.

The limited chorus-lines made up by girls who tried to get their own acts together, were thin, and only occasionally established themselves in the public eye. Even acts which aimed specifically at titillation were relative failures, though there were a good many of them, for a time: Les Parisiennes, for instance, the Ballet Plastique Issatchenko (whose speciality was a kind of erotic Indian dancing), and Les Chattes, in their

topless ballet tutus. Then there were acrobatic dancers, often originally acrobats, who had learned dance routines into which were woven acrobatic feats, using the supposed convention of the gymnasium or sometimes a neo-Grecian setting, to appear practically naked, and reminding one of the then extremely risqué Aretino etchings.

In the 1970s, it can probably be said with some justice that when a chorus girl dies she no longer goes to Paris, but to Las Vegas, where the pay is better and the shows more opulent. The Folies, compared even with some of the shows available in London, let alone off-Broadway, seems old-fashioned, and the other night-spots can no longer compete, financially, with the most ambitious American productions. At the Lido or the Crazy Horse Saloon, hints of the once-supreme Paris chorus-line still remain, but the main glory is departed; the Parisian chorus girl no longer leads, but follows.

And yet . . . and yet . . . Paris had such a good start! For so many years, the naughty French novel, the naughty French play, the supreme naughtiness of the French can-can, and of course the Folies, was the lure which took every young man who could possibly afford it on his first trip abroad—and the glamour will never quite fade. It is difficult to imagine a time when the Folies Bergère will bring a final curtain down on its lines of splendidly-decorated girls, or when the last *cache-sexe* will be hung up with the last pair of ballet slippers.

A stunningly elegant scene at the Paris Lido: one nude dancer supported by a single man and 14 girls in splendid costumes—every face that of an individual

4 The
Gaiety Girl

'Ladies drawing less than 25s a week are requested not to arrive at the stage door in their private broughams.'

John Hollingshead

The Gaiety Girl, who flourished between the late 1860s and the end of the first decade of the twentieth century, was possibly the most famous chorus girl of all time: not even the Ziegfeld Girl or the Cochran Young Lady was as well known, as sought-after. No-one spoke of The Daly's Girl, The Prince of Wales's Girl, or The Opera Comique Girl. The Gaiety Girl was the essence of musical theatre, and became a legend.

John Hollingshead, the builder and first manager of the Gaiety Theatre in London, really created her. Planning the opening shows for his new theatre, in 1868, he looked for success to his stars—above all the enchanting Nellie Farren—but he also selected a small chorus and an even smaller *corps de ballet*. He decided right from the start to concentrate on beauty.

'My view of the stage,' he once wrote, 'was that whatever it might be, judged from the lofty, not to say stuck-up heights of Literature and Art, it was not a platform for the display of grandmothers and maiden aunts. If physical beauty could be got in combination with brains and dramatic talent, so much the better, but my first duty seemed to me to be to get physical beauty, and I got it.'

There were plenty of theatre choruses in the London of his day whose beautiful voices emanated from dumpy ladies with plain faces. Hollingshead made sure that every girl who set foot on the stage of the Gaiety was a beauty; if she could sing well, that was a bonus—but he believed very simply that the larger number of pretty girls on his stage, the less the audience would care if the musical noises they made were a little weak. Equally, his dancers must all have good figures and pretty faces; if they could dance well, that again was a bonus—but the shapeliness of their legs was on the whole more important than their agility.

Occasionally, girls whose beauty was matched by their voices were found. W. S. Gilbert, conducting a rehearsal at the Gaiety, was once approached by a minor principal who complained that she was not being given enough to do. 'Why should I just stand here?' she asked. 'I am not a chorus girl.' 'No, madam,' replied Gilbert, 'your choice is not strong enough, or no doubt you would be.'

The entertainments presented at the Gaiety, the Alhambra, the Folly and the Royal Strand theatres in London in the 1860s and 1870s were generally considered rather *risqué*, and so attracted moderately disreputable (if harmless) audiences. The girls on-stage were not 'ballet-girls', but concentrated on simple and unaffected 'numbers'—even skirt-dances were considered too sophisticated for the audiences. Hollingshead called himself, frankly: 'A licensed dealer in legs, short skirts, French adaptations, Shakespeare, taste and the musical glasses.'

The girls at first wore tights, while the men often wore costumes which were variations on the eccentric clothes of the *commedia dell'arte*, though later both men and girls became, almost, fashionable models.

Previous pages: Girls from the Gaiety Theatre, dressed in finery which George Edwardes provided at great expense for them to wear 'in society'

Opposite: The Gaiety Theatre, London, opened on December 21 1868 by John Hollingshead: the five rows of stalls gave way to a pit with backless benches; 2000 patrons crowded in, 500 of them to the gallery

When George Edwardes began to present genuine musical comedy for the first time at the Gaiety, after Hollingshead's retirement, the chorus appeared in the street clothes of the period, in Savile Row suits and beautifully cut, specially designed dresses.

The Girls came from every sort of background, and were equal only in beauty and talent, both of which were considerable. Hollingshead's eye was for character as well as beauty, and his girls were celebrated not 'only' for their looks. When, early in his reign, tights and ballet skirts became old-fashioned, he still dressed his Girls to show off their figures: very little bare flesh was to be seen, but the costumes were close-fitting, and it was evident to the eye that there was not much of them. (There is nothing so erotic as the girl who can be seen to be naked beneath her clothes.)

The chorus had no choreography as we would understand the word; yet they were more than *mannequins*. Described in the programmes as 'society ladies' or 'friends' of the leading lady (in musical plays) they reacted to what was going on about them, and each was allowed to be individual in her reactions. The complete uniformity of appearance and movement which was to be the fashion half-a-century later was unthought-of, as was the vulgarity of a line of high-kicking girls which is our idea of the typical 1930s chorus.

The Gaiety Girl had not suffered the agony of a long classical ballet training; she may not even have come up through the rigours of pantomime. She had to be able to walk well, move elegantly, and wear expensive costumes with dignity and poise. In a sense, *the chorus*, at the Gaiety, were choristers—ladies who sang their hearts out, unseen, behind a convenient 'flat'. The Girl, meanwhile, sat (beautifully) while the star did a number—perhaps moving an elegant arm in time to the music, pointing a neat foot in one direction, then another, and walking sinuously around the stage. Nothing very demanding; nothing requiring years of training, concentration, pain.

But what the Girl had to do, she had to do extremely well, and with the greatest possible style. And there was a sharp division between her 'dancing', and the dancing of the girls of 'the ballet'; later, apart from leading dancers, they became almost one and the same; but at the time when the Gaiety was gaining its reputation, the dancing choruses at other theatres had considerable shortcomings; their beauty was often matched not by their technique but by their frills and feathers.

Bernard Shaw, while drama critic of *The Saturday Review*, let himself go on the subject of dancing in the issue of 9 January, 1897, in which he reviewed the new production of Huan Mee's *A Man About Town*, 'a musical farce' with a score by Alfred Carpenter, at the Avenue Theatre.

Four Gaiety Girls on postcards, displaying costumes from the discreetly erotic to the mock-historical, the semi-circus to the vaguely continental. The photographs are c. 1880

'The perfect dancer', he pointed out, was one thing; but 'the stage is always liable to the incursions of beauteous persons whose misfortune it is to be unable to dance at all, and who suffer from a similar disability in respect of singing or acting. Some excuse being necessary for the exhibition of their charms on the boards, an unskilled accomplishment had to be invented for them. And this was the origin of the skirt-dance, or dance which is no dance, thanks to which we soon had young ladies, carefully trained on an athletic diet of tea, soda-water, rashers, brandy, ice-pudding, champagne, and sponge-cake, laboriously hopping and flopping, twirling and staggering, as nuclei for a sort of bouquet of petticoats of many colours, until finally, being quite unable to perform the elementary feat, indispensable to a curtsey, of lowering and raising the body by flexing and straightening the knee, they frankly sat down panting on their heels, and looked piteously at the audience, half begging for an encore, half wondering how they would ever be able to get through one.'

The girls got away with this, Shaw suggested, because the audience 'felt the charm of the petticoats, and was mean enough to ape a taste for the poor girls' pitiful sham dancing, when it was really gloating over their variegated underclothing.' What one got, in musical plays of the period (Shaw suggested), was a mixture of these 'altogether incompetent professional beauties', 'ambitious ballet-girls', 'step-dancers from the music-halls'—'the result, up-to-date, being a dance which is a mixture of cheap *pas seul* with the sort of kick-up a music-hall "serio-comic" ends her turn with.'

Max Beerbohm, a less acid critic, has left a glimpse of the Gaiety Girl at roughly the same period, which shows the distance Hollingshead and later George Edwardes were able to set between them and their less statuesque sisters elsewhere. Beerbohm was reviewing *Our Miss Gibbs* at the Gaiety:

'As always,' he wrote, 'the surpassing delight is the chorus. The look of cold surprise that overspreads the lovely faces of these ladies whenever they saunter on to the stage and, as it would seem, behold us for the first time, making us feel that we have taken rather a liberty in being there; the faintly cordial look that appears for the fraction of an instant in the eyes of one of them who happens to see a friend among us—a mere glance, but enough to make us all turn with servile gaze in the direction of the recipient; the splendid nonchalance of these queens, all so proud, so fatigued, all seeming to wonder why they were born, and born so beautiful . . .

Left: **Five fairies from a Gaiety burlesque of 1884. Above: The Belle of New York (1898). Below: at the Gaiety: a seaside scene, and the famous Pas de Quatre from** Faust-up-to-Date **(1888)**

I remember that when [in 1898] *The Belle of New York* was first produced in London every one prophesied that the example of that bright, hard-working, athletic American chorus would revolutionise the method of the chorus at the Gaiety. For a while, I think, there was a slight change—a slight semblance of modest effort. But the old local tradition soon resumed its sway, and will never be over-thrown; and all the Tory in me rejoices.'

The Gaiety Girls.

SOME PRETTY STUDENTS AT GOTTENBERG COLLEGE

MISS
CISSIE
MURRAY

MISS
DORA
FRASER

MISS
MAY
CHARTERIS

MISS
BLANCH
BROWN

MISS
GERTRUDE
WYKES

MISS
CONNIE
STUART

MISS LILY SHEPHERD

35

58

The American influence was felt elsewhere: within fifteen years, producers were making great efforts to import the vivacity and novelty of the American style. At the London Opera House in 1913, for instance, the producers of *Come Over Here* secured an Anglo-American chorus, and the press department suggested that patrons would have the best of both worlds:

'The American girl relies upon her vivacity, her
boldness, her swinging gait, and her suggestion of
independence in winning the man she loves. The English
girl, on the other hand, is softer, more delicately
seductive, more daintily alluring. In the heart's
depth, one is as firm and strong as the other; but
the English girl gives the Englishman the impression
that she is more intensively feminine than her American
cousin.'

The Gaiety, however, continued to rely on its old style, though making a very few concessions to modernity. Titillation without offence was the motto: high-kicks for instance were available, but regarded as vulgar. 'In high-kicking there is absolutely no merit,' wrote one critic. 'It is mere gymnastics—an accomplishment which (granted the possession of sufficiently long limbs) can be acquired by patience without any aid from brains. It is ungraceful, and it is vulgar. Dancing, it certainly is not. It is admired and applauded by many; but by those artists who respect themselves it should be rigorously tabooed.'

The Girl at the Gaiety became a star in her own right by a combination of virtues; and even when her name was unknown to her audience, there was no doubt of her status—her stardom was reflected, for instance, in her adoption as a photographic model in the early days of the camera. Before the picture-postcard era, she could be snatched from the stage and immortalised in a cabinet photograph (for which she received little, if any, payment). One of the early Girls actually starred in a religious photograph entitled *Rock of Ages*—though it is doubtful whether the curates who bought that picture were aware of the provenance of the model.

George Edwardes' first experimental musical comedy was staged at the Prince of Wales Theatre in 1892. *In Town* was an anecdote about a young man-about-town who invited the young ladies of the Ambiguity Theatre to lunch, and then found he could not pay the bill. He was rescued by a young lord, whose noble parents discovered him surrounded by girls.

In Town was a considerable success, and a journalist commented on the magnificence of the staging, and the 'very, very smart frocks . . . worn by the "chorus ladies" of the Ambiguity Theatre in the first act.' The Ambiguity Girls were true precursors of the Gaiety Girls at the height of their influence; it was only a year later that *A Gaiety Girl* opened at the Gaiety itself; and in four years' time a correspondent of *The Sketch*, having seen *The Shop Girl*, was able to declare:

In 1907, George Edwardes produced The Girls of Gottenberg at the Gaiety, with Gertie Millar, George Grossmith, and a supporting cast including the young ladies opposite – each a distinct individual, from the tentative, slightly shy Miss Murray to the open, charming Miss Stuart

A Gaiety Girl (opposite) was produced at the Prince of Wales's in 1893, but transferred to Daly's after an enormous success. One of the girls in the autographed illustration, Blanche Massey, had been in In Town, produced a year earlier at the Prince of Wales's, as an Ambiguity Girl. In Town, 'a musical farce', was the first real musical comedy

'The stage of the Gaiety Theatre is to the very modern *genus* "Johnny" at once a Mecca and a feast of Tantalus. This is wicked "derangement of epitaphs", as Mrs Malaprop would have said, but it can be justified. The Gaiety stage is the masher's Mecca; his eyes are continually turned towards it, and yet he is always kept from the idols of his heart by a few yards of intervening space. Herein lies the suggestion of Tantalus, which I forbear from amplifying. Nightly the worshippers beset the shrine of the Sacred Lamp, and on the stage the maidens whisper that What's-his-Name is in front again this evening . . .'

Tantalus occasionally obtained his reward. The other Girls used to tease one of their number when they discerned the bald head of an admirer shining in the front row of the stalls. But eventually she did become the Duchess of Leinster.

The Sketch's representative was somewhat disappointed when he finally managed to obtain permission to go backstage:

'From the front, several of the dresses, or suggestions of dresses, looked somewhat daring, but on the stage they appeared quiet enough,' he complained. 'There was such a thoroughly business-like air about proceedings . . . that a Sunday School meeting, or a prize-distribution at a girls' school, could not have been more free from offence.'

Matinee every Saturday at 2.30.

Matinee every Saturday at 2.30.

PRINCE OF WALES THEATRE.

Proprietor of Theatre   Mr. EDGAR BRUCE.

Licensed by the Lord Chamberlain to Mr. GEORGE EDWARDES, 6, Park Square, West, Regents Park.

On SATURDAY, OCTOBER 15th, and Every Evening at 8.30,

Will be produced the New Musical Farce, in Two Acts, entitled

IN TOWN

By Messrs. ADRIAN ROSS & JAMES LEADER.   Music by F. OSMOND CARR.

IN WHICH

Mr. ARTHUR ROBERTS and Miss FLORENCE ST. JOHN.

WILL APPEAR

Captain Arthur Coddington		Mr. ARTHUR ROBERTS
The Duke of Duffshire		Mr. ERIC LEWIS
Lord Clanside	(his Sons)	Miss PHYLLIS BROUGHTON
Lord Alexander Kincaddie		Master DOUGLAS PATRICK
Rev. Samuel Hopkins	(his Chaplain)	Mr. E. BANTOCK
Benoli	(Manager of the Caravanserai Hotel)	Mr. H. GRATTAN
Hoffman	(Hall Porter at the Caravanserai)	Mr. FRITZ RIMMA
Fritz	(Head Waiter at the Caravanserai)	Mr. E. FRAZER
Mr. Driver	(Stage Manager of the Ambiguity Theatre)	Mr. F. LOVELL
Shrimp	(Call Boy at the Ambiguity)	Miss JENNIE ROGERS
Bloggins	(A Solicitor's Clerk)	Mr. VAUGHAN
The Duchess of Duffshire		Miss MARIA DAVIS
Lady Gwendoline		Miss BELLE HARCOURT
Lady Evangeline		Miss D. GILPIN
Flo Fanshawe	(Principal Dancer at the Ambiguity)	Miss SYLVIA GREY
Bob		Miss MAUD HOBSON
Billie		Miss BLANCHE MASSEY
Lottie	(Ambiguity Girls)	Miss HETTY HAMER
Lillie		Miss N. SIMMONDS
Clara		Miss K. CANNON
	AND	
Kitty Hetherton	(Prima Donna of the Ambiguity)	Miss FLORENCE ST. JOHN

Waiters, Guests, Chambermaids, Burlesque Actors and Actresses, &c.

All the Music of this Musical Farce is published by JOSEPH WILLIAMS, 24, Berners Street, W.

Scene.—Act I.		Vestibule of the Caravanserai Hotel.	(Banks).
Act II.		Green Room of Ambiguity Theatre.	(Telbin).

Produced under the Direction of J. T. TANNER.

The Costumes for the Travestie of "Romeo and Juliet" in Act II., designed expressly by WILHELM, and executed by Miss FISHER, AUGUSTE ET CIE, and J. A. HARRISON, Limited. Modern Costumes by HOWELL & JAMES, &c., &c. Wigs by W. CLARKSON. Furniture by LYON.

Preceded at 8 o'clock by

The White Lady.

Box Office open daily from 10 to 6. Doors open at 7.30. Commence at 8 o'clock.
PRICES OF ADMISSION—Private Boxes £1 1s. to £4 4s.; Stalls, 10s. 6d.; Balcony Stalls, 7s. 6d.; Balcony, 6s.; Upper Circle, 4s.; Pit, 2s. 6d.; Gallery, 1s.

| Musical Director | SIDNEY JONES | Treasurer | E. MARSHALL |
| Business Manager | | F. J. HARRIS | |

An American Bar is now opened in the Stalls Foyer of this Theatre.

Business-like, no doubt; but one of Edwardes' difficulties was that the Girls knew their worth, and were sufficiently individual and spirited to make discipline something of a problem. There is, for instance, the story of one who was particularly prone to gossiping with her neighbour on-stage, while the principals were trying to hold the attention of an audience already too prone to concentrating on the Girls. Seymour Hicks eventually lost his temper, and one night in the middle of a song held up his hand to quieten the orchestra, turned to the Girl, and said: 'Dear lady, will you finish your story, or shall I finish my song?'

There was a silence; the Girl's colleagues, and the audience, were aghast for her. But she simply looked Hicks straight in the eye, and said: 'Do you know, dearie, it's a matter of the utmost indifference to me what you do?'

Another Girl, engrossed with a new admirer, failed to turn up for a performance, sending a telegram explaining that she had burned much of her hair off while curling it. Three days later, when she did appear, the stage-manager sent for her, asked to see the burnt hair (which did not exist), pondered for a moment, and then said: 'Well, it is too much to expect it to have re-grown within three days. Perhaps you had better stay at home and let it grow for the remainder of the run of the play; then if it has returned to its full length, we may perhaps re-engage you for the next production.'

The besieging of the stage-door, when the Gaiety Girl was at her most voluptuously attractive, made the stage-door-keeper's job an arduous one; and the Gaiety did attract a succession of almost legendary stage-door-keepers. There was George Moore, the first of the line, who sat surrounded by pictures of his Girls, determined to allow no-one back-stage who had not been invited by the management. He died sitting by the door, after sixteen years in the job. His successor, Tierney, was not adamantly opposed to receiving a sovereign from a stage-door Johnny; but it did not guarantee admission! A lugubrious man, he would deliver his monologue in a slow, repetitive grumble:

'No, sir, you can't go through—I say you can't go though. It's against the rules—against the rules. Nobody ain't allowed through the stage door—I say, nobody ain't allowed through the stage door.'

Tierney's successor, James Jupp—an ex-Sergeant Major of the King's Royal Irish Hussars—was engaged by Edwardes in 1892, and became the Gaiety's most famous stage-door-keeper. With a formidable moustache and an equally formidable voice, he ruled the stage-door with an iron discipline. But he is said to have made a fortune in tips, and to have been able to discriminate faultlessly between the moon-calf poverty of a fashionable young man crying for a glance from a Girl's bright eye, and a young heir to a title whose intentions might be, or might be persuaded to be, more or less honourable. That some young men did buy their way through the door, or at least buy a place sufficiently at it, is indicated by a notice that Hollingshead was forced to

THE GAIETY LANCERS

BY

FRED. GODFREY.

LONDON S.A. CHAPPELL 45. NEW BOND STREET
Military Musical Instrument Warehouse

THREE ACTS IN THE LIFE OF A DANSEUSE.

"I must see you again, Gerty." [See Page 536.

Opposite: A poster designed by Carlobali for the Ambassadeurs, Paris. Miss Campton appears 'toute nue', but seems uncharacteristically coy, even for 1900

place on a board at the Gaiety: 'Ladies drawing less than 25s a week are requested not to arrive at the stage door in their private broughams.' Honourable appearances must be maintained.

Bouquets, presents, visiting-cards, *were* allowed past Sergeant Jupp, and were welcomed by the Girls. As the Duchess of Leinster put it in a broadcast:

'It was a wildly glamourous life, I suppose, in
the way that people used to get to know you, especially
young men, naturally; but I don't think they succeeded
much—they usually took somebody out that was easier
to get to know. They could leave their name at the
stage door; but it was rather difficult with me, you see,
because I had my old nurse who used to go back with me.'

Unprotected by nurse, other Girls certainly made their appearances at Rule's or Romano's, at Jimmie's or the Continental. The supper-room at the Continental, indeed, was for a time the place where anyone went who wanted to catch a glimpse of a Gaiety Girl off-stage. There, after the show, with other less respectable ladies at other tables (though only the most expensive of them), the Girls would be taken by better-off Johnnies; if champagne *was* ever drunk out of slippers, the Continental provided a setting for that somewhat unsanitary form of tribute.

The Girls had other outings. Constance Collier used to tell the story of a time when, at sixteen, with a tiny part in the current show, she received with all the other Girls an invitation to a party at the Savoy. Miss Collier, whose tiny role was rewarded by an equally tiny salary, had nothing to wear to such a fashionable venue. But next evening, she found laid out in her dressing-room an evening dress, a matching cloak, petticoats, stockings, gloves and a fan—all provided by a collection taken up by the other Girls. Later, at the Savoy, she found under her plate (as did all the others) a bundle of £50-worth of South African mining shares.

The glamour of the Girls (spurious only in the sense that they actually worked very hard for a living) strongly affected the gentlemen in the stalls (that was why, after all, the Girls were there); and while the story of the chorus girl who married the *peer* is a cliché, it did happen —more often perhaps to a star than a chorus girl. Perhaps the most famous theatrical peeress was the beautiful Gertie Millar, born in Bradford, a girl babe in pantomime at the age of twelve, who became at the age of 44 the Countess of Dudley. But Gertie Millar was never a chorus girl, though for six years she was a member of a touring choir.

However, Denise Orme stepped from the chorus of *Our Miss Gibbs* to marry the Hon. John Reginald Lopes Yarde-Buller, and eventually to change her name for the third time (she was originally Jessie Smither) and become the Baroness Churston. Sylvia Storey, in the Gaiety Chorus for *Havana*, married the fabulously wealthy Earl Poulett during the run of the show; Olive May married Lord Victor Paget, and later became the Countess of Drogheda.

During the run of *A Gaiety Girl*, eighteen members of George Edwardes' company are said to have left to get married, and when he looked about him he realised that the Countess Ostheim, Lady George Cholmondely, the Countess Torrington, the Marchioness of Headfort and the Countess of Suffolk—and of course Lady Churston, the Countess Poulett and Lady Victor Paget—had all originally been stars or chorus girls under his management. The realisation shocked him into writing a clause into his contracts, applying to the Gaiety, Adelphi and Daly's theatres, in which it was clearly stated that the artiste would *not* be released from the company during the run of any show, for the purposes of matrimony.

Edwardes was not only concerned with the possibility of losing his Girls, but with the fact that once a Girl was married, she lost something of her appeal to the men in an audience (the same attitude was taken when, years later, some male pop-stars dismayed their fans by marrying).

'It's sheer ingratitude!', Edwardes would wail.
'I've done everything for that girl—taught her to
pick up her *h*'s, clean her finger-nails, had her
teeth seen to, her appendix removed, her hair dyed,
dressed her from her underclothes to her boots,
taught her to walk . . . and now, when she's making
good, she *marries*!'

Right: Gertie Millar and a diminutive chorus of boy sweeps in The Orchid, **which opened the new Gaiety in 1903. The Prince of Wales sent a telegram: I'VE LOVED THE GAIETY, I LOVE YOU, AND I LOVE THE GIRLS . . .'**
Far right: The Gibson Girls in The Belle of Mayfair, **at the Vaudeville Theatre, 1906, parasols inverted: very fashionable, very grand**

One Girl remembered receiving her notice three days after quietly marrying. She stormed in to see the Guv'nor (as Edwardes was always called). 'But the boys get to know of it, my dear,' he argued. The Girl pretended to be astounded that the Guv'nor was only interested in her to the extent that she attracted 'the boys'. Surely it was her acting ability, her beauty, that had interested him? Surely her private life was her own, and he would rather she was married than that she gave out her favours to any Tom, Dick or stage-door Johnny?

Edwardes (always susceptible) capitulated at once. His Girls knew how to catch him on the raw. He *was* preoccupied with the reputation of his theatres. He even paid for cabs to bring the Girls to the stage-door, so that they should not arrive on foot, to be accosted by anyone who was hanging about. When a divorce case involved one of his Girls, then a breach of promise action, he became most concerned (especially as the latter case involved a peer). Again, the Girl in question appealed to his sensibilities, and he ended up fighting the case for her, and obtaining damages.

There is another well-documented story that he gave a girl and her mother tickets for a round-the-world cruise, when it was discovered that she was suffering from tuberculosis.

It is doubtful whether Edwardes ever really disliked the idea of one of his Girls marrying a peer, becoming, as someone put it, 'one of the actressocracy', however much he may have been inconvenienced. The publicity was worth far more than the inconvenience. It is doubtful too whether the aristocracy was much harmed, despite the fuming of noble parents. As Pinero (or one of his characters) put it: 'The musical comedy girls will be the salvation of the aristocracy in the country. Just think of them—keen-witted young women, full of the joy of life, with strong frames, beautiful hair, and healthy pink gums, and big white teeth . . .'

ries 2087. THE BELLE OF MAYFAIR. Davidson Brothers
London

"Nuits de Folies"

ALEC
SHANKS
'32

Opposite: One of the designs of
the English artist Alec Shanks
for the Folies Bergère in 1932:
the revue was Nuits de Folies.
The splendour of the headdresses is characteristic. Erté
has designed many costumes for
revue over the past half-century:
here (right) is a design for Le
Tabarin, made in 1938, an
almost heraldic tableau in which
two rather sexless figures
'present' to the audience a
stylised mannequin nue. The
'Restoration' wigs of the outside
figures give them a somewhat
decadent air.

Below: Souvenir postcard
making use of Percy Anderson's
costume designs for San Toy,
produced at Daly's in 1899

The less discerning or keen-witted Girls sometimes took a toss: young men were not always what they seemed. One girl, deluged with expensive presents by an Italian count, eloped with him; but he vanished with all the presents after a few weeks and left her destitute. Edwardes took her back—not as one of the Girls, but as a leading lady for provincial tours.

One tends to think of 'the chorus girl' as one of a large group. But smaller groups of girls have occasionally stepped forward, not always to become stars, but to perform a particular number which has made a success. This happened, for instance, at the Gaiety in *Faust-up-to-Date*, a burlesque which was produced in 1888, and which introduced a *Pas-de-Quatre* to music by Meyer Lutz, a popular Gaiety conductor and composer. Lilian Price, Florence Levey, Eva Greville and Maude Wilmot danced forward in low-cut tight-fitting bodices, frilly petticoats under short, blue skirts and little white aprons. Their black-stockinged legs tripped through John d'Auban's choreography, and the dance became the rage of the town.

Later, and more familiarly, there was, or were, 'The Big Eight', as a journalist dubbed them, forming the centre-piece of many a scene: Maud Hobson, Hetty Hamer, Constance Collier, Maud Hill and the other stately, poised Girls moved with great grace on the stage, carefully trained in movement by specialists engaged by Mr Edwardes.

He knew, particularly, the value of setting the beauty of his Girls in marvellous costumes, and always spent a great deal of time—and sometimes a great deal of money—on them. In *Our Miss Gibbs*, the hats worn by the show-girls cost sixty guineas each, and were brought down for each performance from a famous hat-shop. The costumes, in Edwardes' shows, perhaps lost some of the daring quality of some of Hollingshead's confections. Edwardes brought skirts down, so that a glimpse of leg was more of a thrill than it had been for a generation, and the garter became a symbol of something ineffably 'naughty'.

The Gaiety costumes were much more in character and even period than those of other theatres. Sometimes they became the talk of the town—as happened with the 1890 production *Carmen-up-to-Data*, in which the Girls appeared as toreadors and Spanish ladies.

1

2

3

'Wilhelm', perhaps the most accomplished of English theatre designers of his time, was the son of a ship-builder (his real name was J. C. Pitcher). His designs for The Merry War

(a comic opera with music by Johann Strauss at the Alhambra in 1882) gave the girls a delicately martial air (1, 2). For The New Aladdin (at the Gaiety in 1906) he provided costumes for two

contrasting waitresses from popular restaurants – the Fullers' Girl and the Lyons' Girl (3); while two Parasol Girls from the same show (4, 5) display his meticulous sense of elegance and 'line'.

4

5

6

Finally, an English Stall-keeper in
Beefeater's costume from the Fancy
Bazaar scene in The Shop Girl (6; Gaiety,
1894), and a Moulin Rouge girl from An
Artist's Model (7; Daly's 1895)

Above: The cover of the
programme for Augustus
Harris' pantomime Whittington
and his Cat at Drury Lane

Below: The gymnasium scene
from The Dairymaids (Apollo
Theatre, 1906)

Above: Dan Rolyat, one of the two outstanding comedians in The Arcadians, at the Shaftesbury in 1909: the girls as Arcadian beauties. Lionel Monckton's and Howard Talbot's music still survives

Right: 'Hello, People! People, Hello!' cry the Gaiety Girls, disposed in and around a prop basket for the delight of readers of the illustrated magazines

At Daly's, where Edwardes presented a long series of musical comedies from *An Artist's Model* (his first, which opened in February 1895) to *San Toy*, *A Country Girl*, *The Merry Widow*, *The Dollar Princess*, *The Count of Luxembourg*, costumes also became a feature. Osbert Sitwell remembered some of them:

'The production of *Les Merveilleuses* at Daly's in November 1906', he wrote in *The Scarlet Tree*, 'had introduced, or at any rate popularised, Directoire dresses. The hats were gigantic now, and covered with ostrich feathers . . . At Ascot, and on the lawns of garden-parties, it was to be noticed that women had at least begun to shed once more the multitude of their garments, had left behind the veilings and feather boas in which we saw them wrapped at Lord's, and were now clad, skin-deep, in tight silks, were sheathed in satin, or wore slit skirts, and silver anklets . . .'

The stages of the more fashionable London theatres began to mirror, or even to set fashion—and the youth and beauty of their choruses set them off perfectly. *The Arcadians*, which ran for 800 performances at the Shaftesbury in 1809/10, was a case in point: in the race-course scene (reproduced, half-a-century later as a novelty in *My Fair Lady*!) the ladies and gentlemen who attentively watched the horses race their way across the back of the stalls, were dressed in the height of fashion—hobble skirts, and their successors, the divided skirt, and every up-to-date accessory. The long run, in fact, meant that the chorus were re-dressed several times, and more than one accessory was not only in, but out of, fashion before the show closed.

Audiences soon expected the chorus to be well-dressed, and while a show-girl before the First World War would only be earning from

£2 10s to £5 a week, her costume would cost a very great deal: at the Empire, she might be wearing a dress costing from fifty to a hundred guineas.

With the task of showing off to the best advantage the clothes she wore, as well as taking part with reasonable conviction in what plot there was to participate in, the standard required from a Gaiety Girl was considerable. Edwardes strictly held to his predecessor's prejudice that grandmothers and maiden aunts were undesirable on his stage. Girls chosen nine months earlier for a particular show would be carefully scrutinised through opera-glasses from a box at a performance, and the stage-manager informed if they were thought to be beginning to look too mature.

Edwardes' judgement in these matters was not purely academic, one is to believe; and he is said to have been assisted in his judgement by no less a connoisseur than King Edward VII, who occasionally pointed out a promising young beauty in the back row of the chorus, whose unexpected promotion shortly afterwards was a surprise to her friends, but not to the King.

A less distinguished connoisseur was Herr Lutz, the conductor, who was never afraid to make his opinion known. ('She is no goot: she squints mit her knees', he was once heard to observe.)

The changes of style, the changes of pace, the changes of taste (in particular of the young men who, on leave from the mud and blood of Flanders, wanted to look at girls rather more lively, extrovert, blood-stirring than the stately Girls at the Gaiety) eventually led to the desuetude of Mr Edwardes' epoch-making choruses. But the Gaiety Girl is immortal: an integral part of the history of the London musical theatre.

Right: A scene from Cole Porter's Aladdin, produced at the London Coliseum at Christmas, 1959, whose vast stage had supported a long succession of big chorus-scenes

Below: Esther Williams at the head of a corps of swimming chorus-girls, while more wait fully-clad on-shore beneath two splendid silver sea-horses. The film was On an Isle with You, an MGM production of the '40s

Below, right: Joan Taylor exhorts a tribe of Indians from the summit of a cardboard mountain in the Totem-tom-tom number from the MGM film of Rose Marie, a decade later

It seems to have been *The Black Crook*, staged in 1866, that set the pattern for the development of musical comedy and the chorus-line in America. It was in essence like an English burlesque—a cross between satirical revue, operetta, ballet and pageant—and was revived eight times within a few years, despite (or perhaps because of) the fact that critics deplored the excess of 'feminine pulchritude shockingly revealed sans all Victorian modesty.'

Well, Americans were evidently fairly easily shockable, certainly outside New York. Mrs Frances Trollope, touring the United States only thirty years earlier, was a theatre-goer:

'Two very indifferent figurantes, probably from the Ambigu Comique, or la Gaieté, made their appearance at Cincinatti while we were there; and had Mercury stepped down, and danced a *pas seul* upon earth, his godship could not have produced a more violent sensation. But wonder and admiration were by no means the only feelings excited; horror and dismay were produced in at least an equal degree. No one, I believe, doubted their being admirable dancers, but every one agreed that the morals of the western world would never recover the shock. When I was asked if I had ever seen anything so dreadful before, I was embarrassed how to answer; for the young women had been exceedingly careful, both in their dress and in their dancing, to meet the taste of the people; but had it been Virginie in her most transparent attire, or Taglioni in her most remarkable pirouette, they could not have been more reprobated. The ladies altogether forsook the theatre; the gentlemen muttered under their breath, and turned their heads aside when the subject was mentioned; the clergy denounced them from the pulpit . . .'

The rot spread slowly from Europe, and spread first, of course, to New York, where Lydia Thompson's British Blondes spread the message of British pulchritude as early as 1868, to be followed ten years later by Emily Soldene's Opera Bouffe Company, which appeared at the Lyceum.

'Never had been seen such girls,' wrote Miss Soldene in her memoirs; 'real girls, with fine limbs, complexions nearly all their own, beautifully creamy white skins, figures perfect, gay, bright, healthy, laughing girls, blonde girls, blonde girls with blue eyes, with demure dreamy grey eyes, soft brown eyes, bright hazel eyes, but they all had black lashes. Then their hair, wonderful hair, running the professional long-haired sisters very closely indeed—yellow, flaxen, red, bronzy, long, crispy, curling and rippling . . . "The Boys" simply went crazy over this crowd of imported loveliness.'

'These orgies of nakedness are disgusting, worse than one can find in the lowest dives in Europe; and they make one ashamed of ever having anything to do with revue.'
Florenz Ziegfeld

DEDICATED TO MISS SOLDENE.

THE DROGAN QUADRILLE.

"MISS SOLDENE AS DROGAN IN GENEVIEVE DE BRABANT" From a Photograph by W. & D. Downey, 9 and 9a York Road

BY
P. W. HALTON.

LONDON: METZLER & C.° 37. G.T MARLBOROUGH S.T W.

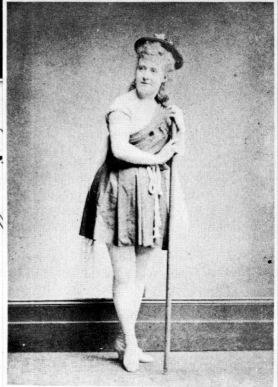

FOUR MEMBERS OF THE " BLACK CROOK " CHORUS: These girl dancers shocked the respectable when they appeared on the New York Stage in 1866 and brought into the box office a million dollars.

"The Boys" were *not* impressed, it seems, by the local equivalent; neither was Miss Soldene: the American girls in the shows she saw in New York were all wearing obviously third-hand costumes bought cheaply in London, with uncared-for shoes and tights; and '75 per cent of the girls don't know how to put their dresses on!'

George Edwardes was quick to follow the lead of the Misses Thompson and Soldene; *A Gaiety Girl*, *The Geisha*, and *A Runaway Girl* all ran successfully in New York, the bright-eyed English girls dealing a death-blow to the rather stolid American girls, many of them acknowledged prostitutes, who appeared on variety bills, in vaudeville and American burlesque—which eventually was to become degenerate and unlovely.

Ironically, it was not to be too long before the American chorus girl proper (who had evidently learned quickly) was to return the compliment. In 1896, *The Belle of New York* arrived in London from New York. American critics had been somewhat half-hearted about that show ('Legs, Lingerie and Vulgarity: Another Casino Production', the *New York Herald* headlined). But London loved it. Half-a-century later, *Oklahoma!* caused a revolution in the British musical theatre, from which it has never quite recovered. The chorus of *The Belle of New York* was ecstatically received in London. *The Era* commented:

'The chorus, who must have to do some hard work
behind the scenes in changing, have plenty of spirit
to spare for their business when on the stage, and do it
most vigorously and smartly.'

The typical American dancing chorus of the 1890s was small, and usually highly-trained (American producers realising that training was one of the English girls' secrets). They often supported speciality or 'exhibition' dancers somehow introduced into the plots of musical comedies. Show-girls ('young ladies', as the programmes often called them) simply added a decorative frieze.

Outside New York, the chorus girl (if she can be dignified with such a title) was pretty rough, and almost invariably ready, up to the turn of the century. At the time when Mr Edwardes' young ladies were setting a new style in New York, less elegant entertainments were promised in the West to gentlemen in search of a little relaxation after a hard day in the mines or on the prairie. Hays City, Kansas, provides a fair sample:

'Hays City by lamplight,' wrote an eyewitness
in the 1880s, 'was remarkably lively, but not very
moral. The streets blazed with the reflection from
saloons, and a glance within showed floors crowded
with dancers, the gaily dressed girls striving to hide
with ribbons and paint the terrible lines which that
grim artist, Dissipation, loves to draw upon such
faces. With a heartless humour he daubs the noses
of the sterner sex a cherry red, but paints under

Opposite, top: Lydia Thompson in Blue Beard **(Drury Lane, 1901)**; left: Emily Soldene as Drogan in Genevieve de Brabant **(Philharmonic, 1871)**. Bottom: four girls from the original New York production of The Black Crook **(1866)**; six years later it reached the Alhambra in London, but ran for only 204 performances

the once bright eyes of women a shade as dark as the
night in the cave of despair . . . To the music of violins
and the stamping of feet the dance went on, and we saw
in the giddy maze old women who must have been
pirouetting on the edge of their graves.'

It is clear that the beautifully produced musical entertainments
provided in Hollywood films for the New Frontiersmen were somewhat idealised. A glance at the history of the West confirmed that the
girl who had the temerity to seek a living on the stages there must have
been tough indeed. Dodge City ('the Queen of the cow-towns', 'the
wickedest little city in America' and 'the beautiful, bibulous Babylon of
the frontier', not to say 'the Gomorrah of the plains') was a paradise for
gamblers long before Las Vegas was thought of. At the Lady Gay
Saloon, Big Nose Kate Fisher's place, or at the Alhambra, rough
cabaret shows were provided by girls who travelled from town to town
with their routines; while The Cosmopolitan Hotel nearby had rooms
which were let by the ten minutes.

Occasionally, a nineteenth century Western equivalent of Miss
Bluebell kept an eye on things. Dora Hand, 'Queen of the Fairybelles'—
dance-hall chorus girls were known as Fairybelles—was said to have
sung in grand opera, and certainly was heard to lead the hymns in
church on Sunday at Dodge City. Until she was shot by mistake by
James W. 'Spike' Kennedy (who was gunning for the Mayor of Dodge
at the time, one Mr James H. 'Dog' Kelley) she maintained a reasonable
degree of order in several halls, though Calamity Jane occasionally
turned up to spit tobacco-juice at any over-brazen chorus-girl.

"DANCE - HOUSE."

It would be a mistake to go too minutely into the behaviour, let alone the routines, of the girls who made their livings in the West before 1900. As soon as the musical got going in New York, tours were sent out, bringing civilised entertainment to most major cities of America. Between them and the strippers of burlesque was a great gulf set.

It was in the new century, and predictably in New York, that the all-American chorus girl was born: less a chorus girl in the classic sense, than a show girl; but in any case the product of the imagination and vision of one man: Florenz Ziegfeld.

Between 1907 and 1931, Ziegfeld presided over the Ziegfeld Follies, and set the standard for revue in America not only by the singularly beautiful stars he promoted—Mae Murray, Marilyn Miller, Lillian Lorraine and the rest—but by over 3000 beautiful girls who at one time or another found themselves, often unnamed but invariably celebrated, in his chorus-line: the Ziegfeld Girls, whose impeccably-drilled and impeccably-styled long legs brought men back again and again to the Follies, often at exorbitant black-market prices ('Diamond Jim' Brady is said to have paid as much as $750 for ten seats at the opening night of a Ziegfeld show).

Ziegfeld had little competition in the field of revue: instead of the twenty or so girls, with two or three changes of costume, at other theatres, he provided a breath-taking cast of a hundred and twenty beautiful, carefully chosen girls with twenty or more changes—and into costumes carefully designed by top-ranking costumiers. Their dancing talent was negligible; as long as they moved well to the music of a large and well-rehearsed orchestra, with plenty of strings, Ziegfeld was happy. And so was his audience.

Opposite: H. B. Bell's 'The Varieties' in Dodge City, c. 1878, presumably on a quiet afternoon: three extremely respectable girls are in the far distance. Respectability enters less into an artist's impression of an Abilene Dance House of the same period (above), where a bunch of the boys are whooping it up, with full orchestral accompaniment

'Ballet girls' in Whirl of the World at the London Palladium in 1924. The term 'ballet' is here loosely employed, as it was in many a programme of revue

The first Ziegfeld Follies opened on 9 July, 1907. It was announced as 'Another One of Those Things, in Thirteen Acts'—which seems modest enough; but Ziegfeld, a pioneer of press publicity as well as of revue, worked away behind the scenes to intimate that this was to be biggest, best, most intimate, suggestive, expensive, beautifully produced show ever to hit New York. He was very possibly right.

Ziegfeld shared one characteristic with Paul Derval of the Folies Bergère: only the best was good enough. He spent money lavishly on his shows. The first Follies cost him $13,000; later he was to spend as much as $300,000 on a single show—big money in the 1920s. Most of it went on costumes, which were always marvellously made; and the girls wore jewellery which was real, the best silks, hip-length silk stockings from Paris (fore-runners of tights).

The girls in the earliest photographs of the Follies seem to us outrageously decorous, dressed in ballet-length skirts and little flowery bonnets, with unrevealing, tight bodices. The show-girls' *décolletage* was a little more revealing, but the girls themselves had a statuesque Edwardian untouchability.

It is evident, however, that the Follies was by no means entirely decorous, for in a famous sleight-of-hand, or sleight-of-eye, in *The Parisian Model*, Ziegfeld produced his first 'nude' scene. In an artist's studio, six girls in long cloaks stood facing a row of easels between them and the audience. Suddenly, they threw off their cloaks, and stood apparently naked for the moment before the lights went out.

Actually, they were wearing strapless evening gowns in a neutral colour, with the skirts pinned up to show their bare legs; but the audience, conditioned by the notion of being in an artist's studio, and expecting a nude, thought it saw one. It was an illusion that seems to have worked night after night, and even lured audiences back for a third or fourth look, long after they must have known what the trick was.

In most of his shows, Ziegfeld promised nudity, but it was only in the occasional tableau that he ever used a naked girl. His girls were almost fully dressed: there was never the degree of nudity which by this time was permitted in Paris. Ziegfeld subscribed to the belief that clothes, properly worn, were infinitely more seductive than nudity—so

sheer silk stockings flashed on the legs of his chorus, and silk covered their perfect figures.

It was a designer called Ben Ali Haggin who persuaded Ziegfeld to take the radical step of using nudes for the first time, in stage reproductions of famous paintings. He announced gravely that nothing was further from his mind than to use the undraped female form to attract men to his theatre. He had decided to represent on stage some of the master-paintings of world art. If one or two of them contained unclad women, then in the interests of accuracy he would feel compelled to include them in his tableaux. And when other producers, who noted that his endeavours in art education resulted in even longer queues at the box office, copied the idea, he rebuked them:

'These orgies of nakedness are disgusting,
worse than one can find in the lowest dives in Europe;
and they make one ashamed of ever having anything
to do with revue.'

Nudity on stage was daring indeed; at first Ziegfeld had to ask for volunteers from the chorus to take part in the tableaux. Miss Kay Laurell occupies a small niche in American theatrical history as the first chorus girl to appear in the US clad in a string of pearls and little else, as September Morn, seated on an enormous globe; and later, standing by the mouth of a cannon, draped in a small corner of a large French flag. Other girls lived to regret that they had not been as forward.

Ziegfeld guarded his beauties well. Very few men ever got past the stage door of the New Amsterdam Theatre to watch as the girls scurried off-stage to the modern elevator which took them up to their dressing-rooms. A girl seen encouraging back-stage visitors was soon rebuked, or even dismissed. But within the bounds of decent behaviour, they were encouraged to publicise the show: and Ziegfeld was the first to use them for that purpose, so that their photographs soon appeared everywhere, and The Ziegfeld Girl became an ideal.

He gave interviews on 'How I Pick My Beauties'. His methods seem perhaps a little eccentric—he would never employ a girl with grey eyes, for instance. They were 'too intellectual, and belong only on a college girl.' In 1917, he was engaging girls with 36 in. busts, waists of 26 in. and hips of 38 in.—he laid great emphasis on the hips; for perfect beauty, he said, they should always be two inches larger than the bust measurement.

When a girl stepped onto the stage in front of Ziegfeld at an audition, he made her stand to attention, the feet together, and made sure that the legs tapered down evenly to the ankles.

'I never diverge from these two rules,' he once said; 'the shoulder-blades, the gluteus muscles of the back, and the muscles of the lower leg must be in direct line with each other.'

Then there was what for a while would have been called 'It': the girls 'must attract men. You cannot define the quality. In one word, I would say it was a promise: a promise of romance and excitement—all the things a man dreams about when he thinks of the word *girl*.'

Perhaps only the Gaiety Girl in Europe was as famous in her own country as the Ziegfeld Girl in America. Ziegfeld was besieged by girls wanting to get into his Follies. He personally auditioned over 15,000 girls a year at the height of his fame—girls from cafés, factories, farms, offices; girls with show-business experience, girls with none. Though the salary was only about $75 a week (not enormous by New York stage standards), there was scarcely a girl in America who would not have rushed to see Ziegfeld if he had sent for her.

The girls shared with the girls of the Gaiety and elsewhere one privilege: that of taking part nightly in a beauty parade attended by

A scene from Irving Berlin's Music Box Revue of 1924. A lady appears to examine her décolletage in a hand mirror, while saluted by two stalwart lady trumpeters whose banners bear the name Thais. She was a Greek courtesan who married an Egyptian King; one would have to find the script of the scene to work out any connection between the visual impression and the legend

some of the most eminently eligible young men in the country. The fact that on their small salary they constantly appeared handsomely bejewelled and in the most expensive furs, hints that Ziegfeld's overseeing of their private lives was broadly interpreted. At the parties thrown for as many of the girls as liked to attend (and there were many of those), gifts of vanity bags containing thousand-dollar notes were taken for granted; there were often emeralds as well.

The one thing on which Ziegfeld did insist was that the girls should be well-groomed whenever they appeared in public. He didn't want, he said, to interfere with his girls' fun; but if he saw one of them in a restaurant without a hat and gloves, high heels and stockings, she got short shrift. The girls were advised to buy one good suit, one good

evening dress, rather than several indifferent ones. Their make-up should be discreet; they should be tidy and neat at all times.

As is always the case, the impression of leisured loveliness hid a great deal of hard work for Ziegfeld's girls. They often worked hard from early morning rehearsal until late night performance; and only then were able to get out with the men of their choice, knowing that the later they stayed out the more difficult it would be to get up for rehearsal next day.

It was legendary that most Ziegfeld girls married millionaires. 'Yes,' the comedian Will Rogers once said, 'every town we hit on tour some of them marry millionaires; but in a few weeks they catch up with us again.' Still, a few of them made very satisfactory marriages; a dozen or so married members of the European nobility, of greater or lesser repute.

In 1929, with the Wall Street crash, Ziegfeld lost a million dollars. His Follies had by now become so expensive that it was almost unthinkable they should ever be started again to less opulent effect. The 1927 show had cost $123,000 for costumes alone; one range of tights sent especially from Paris for the legs of the chorus accounted for $2,329.

Smiles, his first attempt to climb back to success, lost over $300,000; *Show Girl* also failed; so did his new *Follies* of 1931. Apart from the increasing financial burden, taste was changing, and the Follies seemed now a little old-fashioned. In 1932, Florenz Ziegfeld died. His office safe contained eleven elastic bands, two five-dollar bills, and a tin

Three successful American shows. **Opposite, above:** The Greenwich Village Follies of 1925, with costume designs by Reginald Marsh and choreography by Martha Graham. **Opposite, below:** Earl Carroll's *Vanities of 1925,* in which see-through costumes surprised the happy stalls. **Below:** a typical 1920s male chorus in the original production of No, No, Nanette!, dressed for—polo?

Girls from **Earl Carroll's** Follies of 1925. **Carroll constantly attempted to out-do his rival Florenz Ziegfeld, commissioning elaborate costumes (near right), and persuading his girls to appear as nearly nude as made no matter (below) usually using mythology as an excuse**

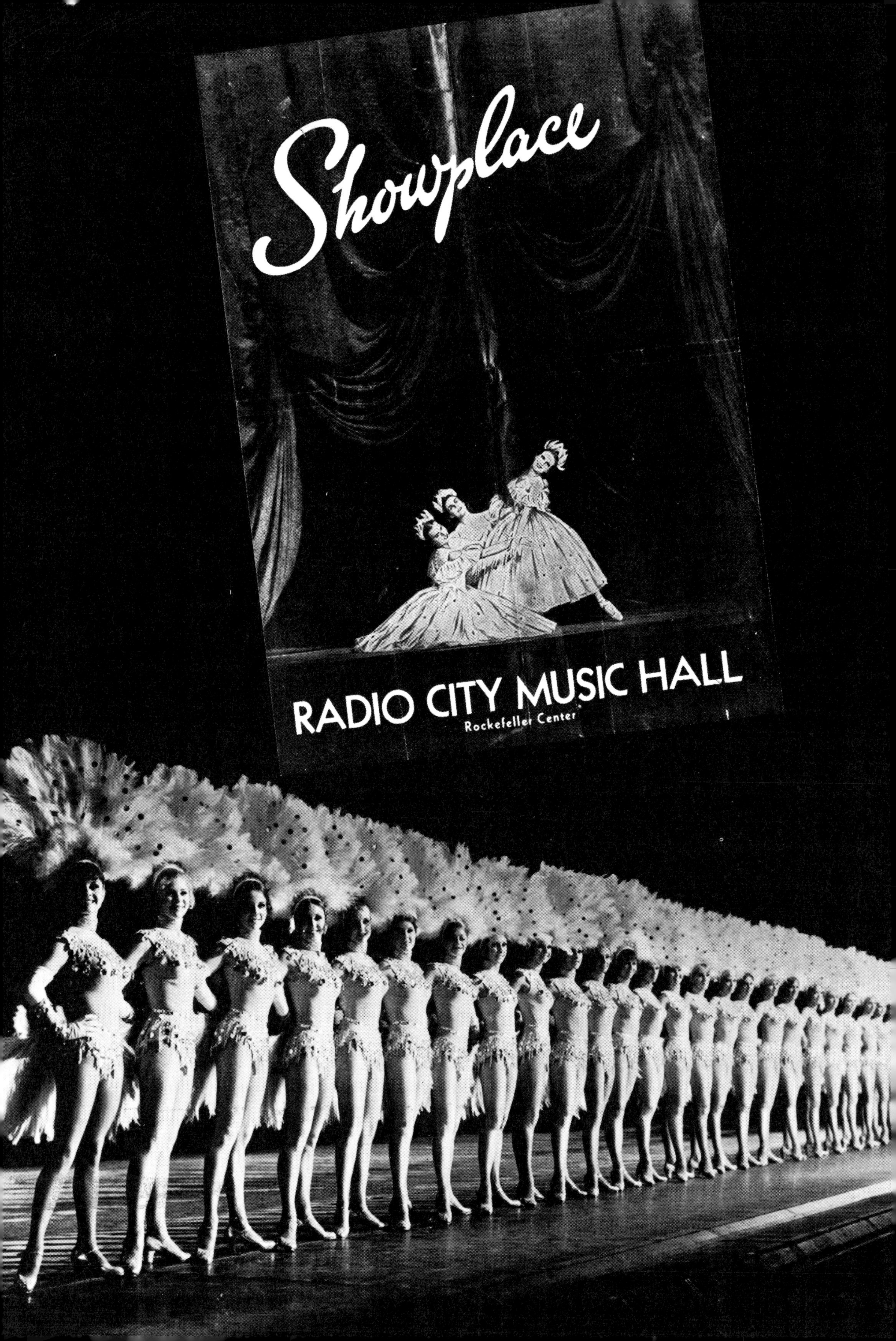
Showplace
RADIO CITY MUSIC HALL
Rockefeller Center

brooch with a large glass ruby. He also left half a million dollars-worth of debts. The Follies died with him.

There were, of course, other impresarios who followed Ziegfeld in his quest for lines of lovely ladies: George Lederer, Raymond Hitchcock, George White and the Schubert brothers—J.J. and his brother Lee, who produced a number of lavish musicals at the Winter Garden Theatre, including an annual revue entitled *The Passing Show*, which was staged every summer (the title 'borrowed' from Lederer). The music, and indeed the sketches, were deliberately subservient to the girls. Preliminary publicity for *The Whirl of the World* (1914) described it as 'An Isle of Gorgeousness, Fun and Music, Entirely Surrounded by Girls. Wherever You Look—Just Girls!' *The American*, reviewing it, wrote:

'Oh, mothers of lads, send your susceptible
ones to *The Philanderer*—or, er, Forbes Robertson;
but keep them, aye, keep them from the Winter Garden!'

Sam Harris and the composer Irving Berlin built The Music Box Theatre especially to stage Berlin's annual revues. *The Music Box Revues* (1921–24) were splendidly garish, and combined this with more taste than ever the Schuberts, or Ziegfeld for that matter, could summon. Alexander Woolcott admired the producers' inventiveness, commented that the girls were never allowed simply to walk on-stage:

'No, they emerge from tree-trunks and bird-
cages, spring up out of trap-doors and lightly
swing down from high trapezes. When this is not
possible they walk groggily down interminable
staircases of black velvet, managing the perilous
descent as nonchalantly as possible under the
circumstances of having to carry with them gowns
of silver sequins weighing about a ton each.'

Very different is the most famous dancing team to come out of America, which was born in 1925 when Russell Markert got together sixteen dancers for a show at the Missouri Theatre in St Louis: he called them The Missouri Rockets. Seven years later, he took a troupe which had grown out of that original chorus to New York, where a vast theatre had been built to hold an audience of 6000 people: The Radio City Music-Hall. The chorus became known as The Rockettes.

They relied—and rely—for their fame on the kind of precision dancing which John Tiller had introduced to European stages many years earlier; in fact one might conjecture that the Rockettes owed their existence to the Tillers, who had reached America when Ziegfeld engaged them for his Follies. But however that may be, their popularity was very great; the line of high-kicking girls became America's idea of what a twentieth-century chorus girl was all about. If it was a glib, somewhat mechanical, and all in all rather debilitating idea, it was none

Above and right: The first all-Negro revue was staged in New York in 1921; in 1928 came the enormously successful Blackbirds, **staged by Lew Leslie, helped along by enthusiasm, slick costumes, and an excellent musical score. The towering golliwogs in the background might now seem offensive, but caused no offence fifty years ago. But of course there would have been few black people in the audience!**

the less immediately seized on by the press and the public (could it have had something to do with the new mechanical age?), and soon the girls who a generation earlier beseiged Ziegfeld for auditions, turned their attention to Radio City.

There are now 46 girls in the troupe, 36 of whom appear on-stage while the rest take a week off; as with every troupe, there are fairly strict height requirements (tallest girl 5 ft. 8½ in.—at the centre of the line, contrary to the European habit—and shortest, 5 ft. 5½ in.—at the ends). There is little that can be said about the life of a Rockette which is not implicit in her work, which is hard (perhaps harder than life in the chorus of a musical, and certainly more boring). Occasionally, very occasionally, there are appearances away from the vast Radio City stage —but the most notable is still as long ago as 1937, when the entire troupe went to Paris for a sixteen-minute appearance at the Exposition —returning with the Grand Prix of the Republic, and three Sèvres vases.

It is difficult, on the whole, not to be reminded when contemplating *chorus girl Americana* as a species, of Paul Derval's opinion: that she is mass-produced, like a Chevrolet or a tin of ham.

'Our methods,' said Derval, speaking of the Folies Bergère, 'are entirely different. Greater stress is laid on the personality of each individual member of a troupe, and I for one am all in favour of this. A

firm believer in the French maxim that uniformity breeds boredom, I select my dancers in the hope that each will claim the attention of a certain number of spectators!' Love one Rockette, and you love them all—and if their popularity seems assured, it is impossible not to connect them in the mind's eye with the interminable procession of cheer-leaders and high-school football-team supporters seen on a hundred campuses.

The Rockettes seem to a European to exemplify the clean-limbed all-American girl at her brashest: each one, no doubt, able to step up front and recite her essay on Why America is Best. Visitors to New York find them as much a part of the scenery as the Empire State Building.

Visitors to Las Vegas, however, watch European girls—and mostly, British girls. The Las Vegas girl has and holds her individual personality (many of them trained by the indefatigable Miss Bluebell, an English-woman who has made Paris her home). More English girls work in Las Vegas than in the West End of London, or perhaps even Paris; they make more money there, and they certainly work hard, with a dis-cipline apparently unmatched by girls of any other nationality. The hundreds of pots of tea gently scenting the dressing-rooms of the MGM Grand, the Dunes or the Stardust hotels fuel some of the shapeliest, most individual and best-paid chorus girls' legs in the world.

6 At Home and Away

For well over a century, the British chorus girl has been much in demand abroad. The European tour became a commonplace for her before the turn of the century, and indeed her popularity in France, Germany, Holland, Italy was mirrored eventually by her vogue in America. The demand in which she has always found herself has not depended on her being more beautiful than her European or American cousins, or even more accomplished; she has simply been, in the long run, more disciplined and a harder worker.

Detailed records of early tours abroad are few and far between, but a Mr Walter Goodman has left a little memoir of a troupe of English girls he happened to come across in Spain in 1885. Señor Moragas had announced a 'real English ballet' for the Teatro del Circo in Barcelona: sixteen young dancers, with 'a few elderly females who acted as their chaperones and "dressers"' all moved into digs in one large boarding-house—except for Little Emily, who was boarded with the British Consul (we are not told why).

Mr Goodman was convinced of the girls' respectability: they 'belonged to a superior order, and exhibited a certain refinement of manner and speech, combined by a steadiness of conduct peculiar to persons who have been well brought up and fairly educated.' However, a group of sixteen-year-olds could scarcely have been expected to live like nuns, and Mr Goodman admits that 'most of them were what is commonly called "lively", and a few were what might equally be termed "frivolous."' They had very little patience with the strange foreign habit the Spaniards had of speaking in an unknown tongue, and Mr Goodman (who for some time acted as their interpreter) was frequently embarrassed at being loudly required to explain to 'this hopeless donkey' or 'that stupid donkey' just what the girls wanted in the way of fruit or vegetables or clothes.

The girls were billed as 'English Blondes—the Pick of the London Playhouses', and while when the curtain rose at the Teatro del Circo it revealed two or three brunettes among a troupe consisting of girls who had fairly obviously little theatrical experience (only one of them had walked onto any stage before, and that in the provinces!) the Spaniards were not disappointed.

'On the opening night there was a perfect *furore*',
Mr Goodman reports, 'when the curtain rose upon *Apolo en el Jardin de Terpsichore*, and displayed the entire strength of the company arranged pyramid-wise, and in graceful poses, upon "bridges" which reached from stage to flies, and extended from the prompt-side to the opposite wing; the apex being formed by a young Spanish dancer who acted as *première danseuse* to the company.'

The season went well.

'The audience were never tired of gazing at my countrywomen as they appeared in the brightest, most

'If you go wrong, go wrong smiling!'
Miss Bluebell

Opposite, above: The 'Beauty Chorus' of The Plantation Revue **company arrives on the SS Albania, 1923**

Below: Bluebell Girls land at Le Bourget in 1937, ready to rehearse for a Follies show with Josephine Baker

99

The playbill for A Gaiety Girl, one of George Edwardes' earliest musical comedies, bears the name Margaret Fraser: Miss Fraser's contract (opposite) with Augustin Daly, a leading American impresario, was for the American tour of 1895, and the Lyceum Theatre was the New York, rather than the London, building

LYCEUM THEATRE PROGRAM

PUBLISHED BY EMIL GROSSMAN & BRO., COR. ST. CLAIR & SENECA STS.

No. 22   WEEK COMMENCING JANUARY 14.   SEASON 1894-95.

ENGAGEMENT ONE WEEK } **Commencing Monday, Jan. 14.**

MATINEES WEDNESDAY AND SATURDAY.

First Production Here of the Reigning Sensation of London and New York,

"A Gaiety Girl."

A Musical Comedy in Two Acts.

Words by Owen Hall.   Lyrics by Harry Greenbank.

Music by Sydney Jones.

CAST OF CHARACTERS.

Charles Goldfield.... ⎫
Major Barclay....... ⎪ Officers   ⎧ ......Mr. Langley
Bobbie Rivers...... ⎬ of the   ⎨ ..Mr. W. J. Manning
Harry Fitz Warren... ⎪ Life   { ....Mr. Bert. Haslem
Ronney Farquhar.... ⎭ Guards.   ⎪ ....Mr. Donald Hall
                                    ⎩ ....Mr. James Fraser
Sir Lewis Grey.............................Mr. Percy Marshall
        Judge of the Divorce Court.
Lance.................... ....Mr. Sinclair
        Goldfield's Servant.
Auguste.............................Mr. Carlton
        Bathing Attendant,
                AND
Dr. Montague Brierly.................Mr. W. H. Rawlins
        Honorary Physician of the Life Guards.

Alma Somerset.... ⎫   ⎧ ....Miss Marion Hood
Cissy Verner...... ⎪ Girls of the ⎨ ..Miss Margaret Fraser
Haidee Walton.... ⎬ Gaiety.   ⎨ .....Miss Helen Fraser
Ethel Hawthorn... ⎪   ⎪ ..Miss Ethel Graddock
Amy Vivian....... ⎭   ⎩ ..Miss Louise Gomersol
Lady Virginia Forest...............Miss Winnifred Dennis
Lady Edytha Aldwyn... ⎫   ⎧ ......Miss Isabel Scott
Miss Gladys Stourton... ⎬ Society ⎨ ..Miss Ethel Maynard
Hon. Daisy Ormsbury .. ⎭ Ladies. ⎩ ....Miss Dolly Kirsch
Lady Grey............................Miss M. Warner
Nina.................................Miss Nina Martino
        Maid to Lady Virginia.
Rose Brierly.........................Miss Ethel Sidney
        The Pas Seul in Act I, Miss Margaret Fraser.
In Act II, a Carnival Dance by Mesdames M. Fraser, H. Fraser and Maude Percy.

100

This Agreement, made and entered into this *twenty eighth of November* 189*4*

by and between *Augustin Daly* party of the first part

and *Margaret Fraser* part *y* of the second part,

WITNESSETH, That the party of the first part engages the exclusive services of the party of the second

part for *about a six months* Tour, commencing on or about *December 25* 189*4*

at a weekly salary of *thirty seven dollars & fifty cents*

Also *with the mutual option of Augustin Daly & Margaret Fraser for*

in of about ten months

For the Season commencing *on or about August 8 1895*

at a weekly salary of *forty dollars*

Also *all railway & steamship fares from London to place of opening &* *with season commencing in America, — with sleepers in case of all night* *journey & all costumes provided*

It is understood and agreed by both parties, that the number of performances to be given each week shall be according to the custom of the place of amusement and city at which *she* may be required to appear, and extra matinées on all legal holidays.

The *party* of the second part engages and binds *herself* and engages *her* full and exclusive services in every respect unto the party of the first part, for the time, terms, and condition stated above; and agrees to aid and assist to the best of *her* ability all performances and rehearsals *as directed* and to act nowhere else in the city of *America & Canada* from the date of this contract until the termination thereof, and to engage in no other business whatsoever while this contract is in force, without the consent of the party of the first part; ~~and to accept two weeks' notification of the termination of this contract as good and sufficient warning of the termination of the same.~~

This engagement holding good until it has been faithfully fulfilled by the party of the second part, or terminated by the party of the first part, as above agreed to, or for infringement of the Printed Rules of the theatre by the party of the second part, which rules are hereby incorporated into this agreement, and so accepted by the party of the second part as part and parcel of the contract.

No performer or other person engaged or employed at this theatre shall be entitled to be paid for any day or days on which the theatre is not opened for theatrical performances on account of any unforeseen calamity or general mourning, or upon any occasion upon which the theatre is closed by law or custom of the country.

The party of the second part agrees that if he shall leave the service of the party of the first part, or act at any other place than that designated by the party of the first part before the termination of this contract, he will pay to the party of the first part the sum of *One hundred pounds* hereby agreed upon as liquidated damages for such breach of this contract.

Margaret Fraser

John Farrington _____ [L. S.]

for Augustin Daly _____ [L. S.]

becoming, and scantiest of dresses, and expressed their
approval by repeated plaudits and costly presents in the
shape of floral wreaths and bouquets in which were often
concealed jewellery, or other articles of value; though
with the exception of the première, it must be confessed
that there was little or nothing in the gyrations to call for
the special admiration of critical spectators well used to the
best examples of the light fantastic.'

In general, it was obviously true that the ladies of the chorus were
only very rarely, if ever, gifted dancers; and even when they were, had
very little interest in dancing *as* a chorus. John Tiller changed all that.

Tiller was born in Lancashire, and had the conventional upbringing
which took him inevitably into the local church choir (of which,
indeed, he became choirmaster by the time he was fourteen). Work with
the choir had the result (perhaps unwelcome in his somewhat strict
family) of making him interested in amateur theatricals, and throughout his early business career in cotton, he remained devoted to the
amateur stage—mainly on the production side, though he took part in
some shows, and there were persistent memories of him blacked-up
with burnt cork as a nigger minstrel.

By the time he was 25, he was said to be one of the richest business-
men in Manchester: a cotton magnate known for generous hospitality,
lively evening parties. But then came the crash: his seat on the Cotton
Exchange became valueless as his business shrank and eventually
vanished. In his 30s, he found himself practically penniless. Fortunately,
he was a man of very considerable imagination, not to say determination; and he turned, at a time when others were desperately floundering,
to his hobby—the theatre.

This chorus of lady cyclists toured Europe (especially Germany) around the turn of the century

ady Cycle Troupe

eauties 12.   Novel

d Cycle act ever produced.

During his visits to the Manchester professional theatre, he had noticed that whatever the virtues of the leading players, the choruses of musical shows, however beautiful, however shapely their legs, spoiled the effect of their numbers by plain lack of discipline. The effect would be much more striking, he thought, if they could be drilled into actually performing the dances as concerted numbers—as a really first-rate *corps de ballet* might.

Though he himself was not a dancer, he persuaded four girls to allow him to try to train them in a new technique, so that all four danced completely together, one mirroring perfectly the movements of the others. In an attic in Manchester the girls thumped through the same routine again and again, until he was happy with the result—'We rehearsed from nine in the morning till twelve at night, and had to walk home in our stockinged feet because they were too sore for shoes,' one of the girls later remembered.

One evening in 1890, the four appeared—billed, excruciatingly, as *The Four Little Sunbeams*—in a show at the King's Theatre, Manchester; and the audience went wild with enthusiasm at their vigorous, carefully-drilled routine. For the first time, an audience clamoured for an encore of a dance routine by a *group* of dancers. Tiller realised that he was indeed on to something good.

Recently, he had married; and with his wife Jennie, he opened a Tiller School in Manchester, holding auditions for students, while his wife found others in the slums of the northern towns (at a time when extreme poverty made the security of a residential school a haven for eight- or nine-year-old girls). Mrs Tiller loved children: while Tiller and some professional dance teachers he had introduced to his methods taught them, she washed them and groomed them and insisted on good behaviour. By the time they were old enough to be sent out on tour, to

THE
TILLER SCHOOLS

LONDON: 143, Charing Cross Rd., W.C.2

NEW YORK: 226, West 72n...

Staff:

LONDON: R. J. Smith,
              Madame Sismondi
NEW YORK: Mary Read
PARIS: Mons. M. Duchard

Directors:

Mr. and Mrs. JOHN TILLER

London, as a Tiller Group, they were attractive, self-possessed young ladies ready to cope with all the vicissitudes of a chorus-girl's life.

By the turn of the century, the Tillers' reputation was growing fast: a London school was opened, and Mr and Mrs Tiller came south to supervise it. Almost every notable musical-comedy was by now turning to them for chorus-girls, and when in 1912 the first Royal Command Variety Performance took place at the Palace Theatre, the 'Palace Girls' all came from Tiller's school.

A strong feature of a Tiller troupe was the family atmosphere which Mrs Tiller firmly instilled: 'Once a Tiller, always a Tiller!' was her word, and she was particularly eager that her girls should be kept from the temptations that were allegedly waiting at the stage-doors of theatres in London and the provinces. This did not mean that she was not delighted when one of her girls got the chance of an advantageous and loving marriage; but she organised a system whereby a troupe Captain—a senior Tiller who had been at the School for some years and was known for her probity and good moral behaviour—looked after any new girls, and kept a good eye on the rest (who themselves were divided into groups of four, with a senior girl responsible for the behaviour of her own group).

The system does not seem to have been too unpleasantly paternal (though no girl would, presumably, stand for it for a moment today). Care was taken that girls who took to each other were allowed to share the same theatrical 'digs' (and those were carefully vetted); while those who showed any signs of jealousy or mutual dislike were kept apart as much as possible. The group leader was responsible for seeing that the other three girls in her group went straight back to the digs after each show, walking determinedly through any groups of 'mashers' or 'johnnies' at the stage-doors. A dim view was taken, too, of any friendships between girls and boys in the same show, if they looked like getting too intense. This was a much greater danger than from outside.

The Captain was responsible for seeing that the girls in her troupe did not drink or smoke too heavily (if only because apart from anything else that would have been extremely detrimental to their stamina). They were encouraged to do their own cooking, especially abroad, where the ravages of unfamiliar food were greatly feared ('*Never* drink the water, dear!'); they often did their own housekeeping, as well as their mending and washing. The Captains had to make weekly reports to the London School, and Mrs Tiller made a special point of keeping in touch with the girls' parents, and letting them know how their daughters were getting on.

The Tillers, apart from their meticulous routines, did much to make the chorus-girl obviously respectable. It was no longer the case that an appearance in a chorus-line automatically branded a girl as having loose morals—though there were of course certain techniques by which the Captain and group leaders could be deceived, and it would be very surprising if every girl in every Tiller troupe returned from a tour quite as virginally dewy-eyed as when she went out. The tours were, after all, often very long, with a frustrating loneliness and lack of social life.

'Once a Tiller, always a Tiller!'

Mrs John Tiller

Opposite: The pawky Palace Girls (below) were trained by the Tiller Schools, as, more obviously, was the quartet of Tillers (above), rather more sedate and ladylike. They were photographed in 1905

105

By the 1920s, lines of Tiller girls were performing in theatres all over England and abroad: Italy, Scandinavia, Germany, South America, South Africa, Australia all welcomed them; a resident group of 48 appeared at the Folies Bergère (the famous 'Les Girls'); Oscar Hammerstein, George White, and Ziegfeld took them to America. It was during a visit to America in 1926, to visit a troupe appearing in the Ziegfeld Follies, that John Tiller died.

Mrs Tiller kept the school running until her own death ten years later, and when she died left her personal fortune to twenty of her girls. The fortune turned out to be £15 at the bank, and a few bundles of pound notes thrown carelessly into the backs of drawers—she had always been extremely generous, and many a girl who had fallen on bad times had been able to count on her help.

But of course there was the school: the training method Tiller had devised, and which had been extended over the years, is still used to train dancers for provincial summer shows and pantomime. Doris Alloway, Barbara Aitken and R. J. Smith, who inherited control of the school, continued to run it as the Tillers would have wished. It would take about three months to turn a competent dancer into a Tiller Girl, and until the 1950s business was still brisk. Pantomime, in particular continued to require annual infusions of Tiller Girls, even after the coming of television had decimated the audience for touring musical shows. Local girls from provincial towns and cities joined professional dancers in Tiller lines for 'panto'—chosen because they had a reasonable ballet technique, or were particularly good perhaps at the traditional Tiller kicks.

There would be perhaps six weeks of 'panto classes' during which new girls would be put through their paces, learning to 'tap' if they had

no experience of that now almost dead art, and 'getting their kicks up' if their legs were not sufficiently loose. Discipline was still fairly tight: a girl could be reprimanded for wearing too much make-up (if she was under eighteen), and hair had to be well-controlled and of a carefully defined length.

The pantomime 'dates' differed in status for the girls: and there were some differences in style, too. A tradition grew up, for instance, that where there was a 'singing fairy' the girls would have to be prepared to take part in a fairly ambitious ballet *scena*, and to go on pointe; if the 'fairy' was a 'ballerina', the girls were less ambitious!

When rehearsals started, the girls allotted to one particular panto-mime would be divided into 'boy-girls' (the taller girls) and 'girl-girls' (the shorter ones). Separate numbers would then be rehearsed, in-cluding that year's speciality—perhaps a straightforward 'kicks' number, or an 'animal' ballet, or even a flying ballet (ten shillings a week extra, as 'danger money', if one flew).

The Tillers were the background of many a provincial pantomime for many a Christmas season, gathering headlines of their own in local newspapers. But there was competition by the 1950s: other schools had followed Tiller's lead, and lines of girls performing high kicks in unison were no longer surprising. And with the coming of television, and a swing away from the touring show (which anyway was beginning to be prohibitively expensive) the Tillers' hold on the world of musical entertainment began to slacken.

There was still—there *is* still, to a limited extent—the summer show, of course: a typical Tiller troupe for summer season at a seaside town might consist of eight girls in their teens or early twenties, each between 5 ft. 4 in. and 5 ft. 8 in., with maybe a couple of dancing boys to

A somewhat teutonic line-up of girls photographed in Paris, c. 1925, with a marvellous variation of expressions behind the monocles

PANTOMIME CHORUS CONTRACT

APPROVED FOR PANTOMIME SEASON 1950/51 AND THEREAFTER

Esher Standard Contract for Pantomime Chorus

RESIDENT OR ON TOUR AT PROVINCIAL AND LONDON SUBURBAN THEATRES. APPROVED BY THE PROVINCIAL THEATRE COUNCIL.

Agreement made this *Twenty third* day of *October*
195*2*, between THE JOHN TILLER SCHOOLS OF DANCING LTD. of
12 OLD COMPTON ST. *Julia Lethbridge*
(hereinafter called "the Manager")* of the one part and
24 Beatrice Avenue of *Lipson Plymouth*
(hereinafter called "the Chorister") of the other part. *(Ply. 61818)*
The conditions set out in Schedules 1 and 2 hereto are a part hereof as though set forth on this page.

TITLE AND LOCATION
Delete whichever not applicable.

1. The Manager engages the Chorister to rehearse and play in the Chorus of the Pantomime entitled *Miss Muffett* and to rehearse and play as understudy such part or parts therein as may be required for a
(a) Resident production at the *Palace* Theatre *Plymouth*.
(b) Tour commencing at the Theatre

Three of these sub-clauses MUST be deleted and initialled by both parties.

2. The engagement shall be:—
(a) Twice Daily.
(b) Twice Nightly.
(c) Twice Daily or Twice Nightly.
(d) Twice Nightly with an Afternoon Matinee Daily (i.e. three times daily)

3. (a) The season or tour shall commence on the *22* day *of December* 195*2* or on some day not more than two weeks before or one week after that date at the discretion of the Manager.
(b) The period of rehearsal shall commence on a day to be appointed by the Manager not being more than *THREE* weeks prior to the commencement of the tour or season.

PERIOD OF ENGAGEMENT
Delete whichever not applicable.

4. The engagement shall commence on the date of the first rehearsal and shall be:—
(a) For the period of rehearsal and the run of the Pantomime subject to one week's notice of termination of such run.
(b) For the period of rehearsal and thereafter until the engagement shall be terminated by either party giving to the other two weeks' notice in writing at any time after the first performance, such notice to expire after the last performance on Saturday, except in the event of the termination of the tour or season when such notice may expire on any other day of the week.

SALARY
Delete whichever not applicable.

5. The Manager shall pay to the Chorister:—
(a) During the period of rehearsal payment in accordance with Schedule 1, Clause A, hereof
(b) From the commencement of the season or tour the sum of £ *5 — 10 —* every week of twelve performances or less which being a salary payable Chorister or Troupe Dancer shall not be less than Five Pounds.
(c) From the commencement of the season or tour the sum of £ every week of eighteen performances or less which being payable under shall not be less than Five Pounds Fifteen Shillings.
(d) From the commencement of the season or tour the sum of £ every week of 12 performances or less which being a salary payable to shall not be less than £3.
(e) From the commencement of the season or tour the sum of £ every week of 18 performances or less which being a salary payable to a under Clause 2 (d) hereof shall not be less than £3.10.0.

LOCAL CHORISTERS

DEFINITION: A LOCAL CHORISTER IS ONE WHO IS RESIDENT IN THE LOCALITY A NORMAL OCCUPATION IS OUTSIDE THE SCOPE OF THE THEATRICAL PROFES WHOSE NAME WILL BE INCLUDED IN A TEMPORARY CERTIFICATE ISSUED TO THE AND COVERING ALL SUCH LOCAL CHORISTERS ENGAGED.

In addition to the salaries provided in (b), (c), (d) or (e) of this Clause the Special Chorister Dancer or Local Chorister shall be entitled to such additional payments as are provided for 6 and the Schedule of this Agreement.

FLYING BALLET

6. Unless specially engaged for the purpose a Chorister shall have the right to refuse to be lif "flying" in a "flying ballet".
A Chorister engaged in flying ballet work shall be paid not less than the sum of 10/- per week for flying and 20/- per week for auditorium flying in addition to the salary stated in Clause 5 hereof.

ARBITRATION

7. Any dispute and questions whatsoever which shall arise between the parties hereto or their respec representatives touching this Agreement or the construction or application of any clause or thing herein contain in any way relating to this Agreement or the affairs dealt with herein or hereunder or the rights, duties liabilities of the parties to this Agreement shall if the parties are unable to agree be referred to two Arbitrator one to be appointed by each party in accordance with and subject to the provisions of the Arbitration Act, 1889, or any statutory modification thereof for the time being in force. One Arbitrator shall be nominated by a recognised theatrical managerial association and the other Arbitrator (to be appointed by the Chorister) shall be nominated by the British Actors' Equity Association or the Variety Artistes' Federation. Provided that this clause shall not in any way affect or restrict the right of either party to this Agreement to apply to the Courts for relief by way of injunction or for an order for specific performance.

e shall expire on
t the Pantomime Class
n November 10th 1952

AS WITNESS the hands of the parties on the day and year first above written.
for and on behalf of
THE JOHN TILLER SCHOOLS OF DANCING LTD. MANAGER*
Doris Allanson CHORISTER
Director,

NOTE: For the purpose of this agreement the Manager may be a Troupe Proprietor or similar, since this contract applies to all types of chorister engaged in pantomimes.

Troupe rehearsals will commence in London on or about December 8th 1952

TELEGRAMS "TIPTOES" WESTCENT. LONDON

12 Old Compton Street
Second floor (Front)

London 5th. October/9 52
W.

...NG

...A AITKEN

...thbridge,
Avenue,

Lethbridge,

Thank you for your letter.

We are holding auditions every Tue...
...n 1 and 2 p.m by appointment - in the...
...Rehearsal Room at 26, West Street, 6...
...idge Circus, W.C.2. We should be ver...
...ee you in relation to the Plymouth Pantomi...
...ou can arrange to come up. If you will say...
...ch Tuesday (the sooner the better) we will gladly...
...e a definite date.

With best wishes,

Yours sincerely,

Doris Alloway

BRITISH RAILWAYS (WESTERN REGION) (6295)

Date   Dec. 14th

RESERVED

FOR

"Little Miss Muffett"

No. of Compts.   4   Class   PARTY
From   Paddn   3rd train 10-30am
Joining   To   Plymouth

750 pads, 100 lvs.—Sec. 38. 1949. (9) S.

Signed ....

Station Master.

Tiller Girls at a music rehearsal
for provincial pantomime, 1952

provide a vestigial male interest. Various dates had their own characteristic tastes: Blackpool traditionally demanded a troupe strong in tap-dancing and the gaudier, brighter routines, while the more sedate Yarmouth or Llandudno were more interested in semi-ballet numbers.

The summer shows were by no means a holiday rest-cure. There were performances only once nightly, admittedly, with two matinées a week; but the programme would be changed every Wednesday, and there would be five different shows, each with every kind of work in it, from the routine high-kicking line to speciality numbers, or 'a nice crinoline number' to support the tenor or soprano in a romantic song. The Tillers would certainly open and close the show.

By now, the Head Girl or Captain was by no means the martinet she had once been—nor so much the mother of the troupe—, though it was certainly her duty to see that the girls rehearsed adequately, that each girl knew the routines she had to perform, and to hand each girl her £6 every Friday afternoon. Not an enormous salary, when one considers the expense of living at a holiday resort at the height of the season (even in not always very salubrious lodgings found in the much-thumbed Equity 'digs book.')

The girls enjoyed themselves, though. There was a tight camaraderie in the company—everyone's troubles being everyone else's. The Tiller organisation continued to keep a personal eye on the troupes, someone from head office turning up at least once during each season. Though the Head Girl was no longer an official informer, scandals had a habit of finding their way to the ears of the London office, and girls involved in any peccadilloes were unlikely to be chosen for the 'plum' jobs—a season at the London Palladium, say, or a tour of South Africa.

South Africa had a voracious appetite for shows from England, and evidently in the 1950s still had much the same attitude to chorus girls as the Londoners of the 1880s. It was the only country where there was still positive trouble with 'stage-door johnnies', and the girls' social life was almost over-catered for; it was rare for a girl to have an evening alone, and invitations to parties and excursions were almost too easily come by. On pay of £11 a week (£5 as a cost of living allowance), and with unlimited hospitality, they lived well in the Johannesburg of 1952. A South African tour was definitely not to be sneezed at.

European tours were of varied quality: they were on the whole hard work, with little reward except the dubious pleasure of seeing other cities. But at least a Tiller troupe was not likely to find itself stranded in Brussels or Berlin when managements failed to meet their commitments, or managers simply vanished.

In one sense, a season at the London Palladium—England's top variety theatre—might have been the height of a Tiller girl's ambition; but it had its drawbacks. Life in London on £8 a week, in the 1950s, was not luxurious, and the work was characteristically hard.

No-one could deny the Palladium Girls looks or ability: but they were as often chosen for their sheer stamina. There were twice-nightly shows, with matinées on Wednesdays and Saturdays. The troupe invariably opened the first and second halves of the programme, and

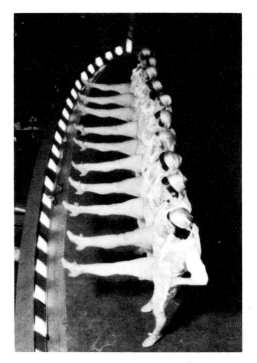

Tiller Girls rehearsing at the Folies Bergère, 1925 (below). Opposite: The Tillers in a boxing scena, at about the same time, also in Paris

sometimes was required by visiting stars to appear as backing to their acts—this was especially true of comedians. After six appearances in one evening, the last of them to close the show, there was little time to pant upstairs to the dressing-room (always at the top of the theatre), hurl oneself out of one's costume, and pelt to the station for a train back to digs, which would necessarily be some way out of town.

The routines were normally changed every other week (unless a star was appearing for a season of three or four weeks, when there was the welcome relief of a longer period dancing the same set-pieces). The week shaped out something like this (with the mornings usually free, to allow for recovery from the night before):

Monday   Band call; first performance of a new
             routine; second performance.
Tuesday   Two performances, with perhaps a rehearsal
             call in the afternoon.
Wednesday Matinée performance; two evening performances.
Thursday Afternoon session rehearsing new routine;
             two evening performances.
Friday   Free afternoon, and weekly pay; two
             evening performances.
Saturday Matinée; two evening performances.

Opposite, above: At the famous
New York Radio City, the girls
open a revue in an uncharac-
teristic, unregimented style. At
Las Vegas (far right), the accent
is sometimes on the individual
show-girl, statuesquely
magnificent in a splendid
costume

Below: the American influence
reaches the Crazy Horse Saloon
in Paris, nipples peeping coyly
from behind somewhat
abbreviated baseball costumes!

It will be seen that the girls received 10s (50 new pence) for each actual performance, ignoring the hours spent in rehearsal! The glamour of appearing at the Palladium must have worn just a little thin under these circumstances, and the pleasure of working with well-known international stars was perhaps no great compensation—the relationship between a star and a chorus-girl is a problematical matter at the best of times; all one can probably hope for is a nod or a wink, and if one receives more it may not always be welcome (there have been cases of the Tiller organisation issuing a proclamation that no girl should go near the dressing-room of a particular star—and not always or necessarily a male star).

The Tillers are not quite so strongly associated with the Palladium as they once were; nor are they so much concerned with pantomime. When in 1973 Robert Smith (who had taken over the organisation in 1936 from Mrs Tiller) retired, the Tiller school was taken over by Robert Luff, with Barbara Aitken remaining as a director and choreographer. The Tiller girls, while still expected to do their famous kicks, are now much more versatile, much more individual; they still take part in a number of English summer shows. But it is to the *history* of the chorus girl that the Tillers have made their great contribution.

A later chapter in that history was written, and is still being written, by one of the great individuals of this story—Miss Bluebell, whose troupes appear at Las Vegas (which has at one theatre the biggest chorus-line in the world, with over 60 girls), the Paris Lido, Buenos Aires, Tokyo, Nairobi, Geneva, Barcelona . . . The Bluebell Girls are as well known now as the Tiller or Gaiety Girls in their day.

Miss Bluebell was 'christened' by an Irish doctor who helped to care for her when as an under-nourished and unhealthy child, she was adopted by a Dublin family (nothing was known of her parents). Mary Murphy, her 'Auntie', brought her to England, when the sickly child began to take dancing lessons with a Madame Cummings (and paid for them by doing some golf caddying and a newspaper round). At thirteen, she got her first stage job; predictably, as a pantomime 'babe', in a production at the West country seaside resort of Newquay. Her salary was five shillings a week, and she sent her 'Auntie' half of it.

Mrs Murphy saw that the stage was clearly the only career Bluebell would be suitable for. At 15, she was removed from school, and joined The Hot Jacks—a little troupe of half-a-dozen girls of the same age who performed mad gyrations in organdie blouses and blue bloomers. From The Hot Jacks, Bluebell made a giant jump to become one of The Jackson Girls, under the aegis of Alfred Jackson (who among other things for some time supplied a permanent group to the Folies Bergère).

Three somewhat stunned 16-year-old girls set out from London for Berlin, and the Scala Theatre. It was 1927. But any idea that Miss Bluebell took any real part in the scandalous night life of the Germany of the 1920s can be dismissed: for one thing, after a day rehearsing and an evening performing the kind of routine The Jackson Girls were famous for (30 girls in a row kicked higher and higher, faster and faster, to the beat of a tambourine) she would have had no energy for it. And

for another thing, Frau Elly, the girls' guardian, marched them to and from rehearsal and theatre in a crocodile formation that would have done justice to the most cloistered girls' school—and watched with an eagle eye over their dormitory.

After six months in Berlin, another six in Leipzig and Essen—and all for two pounds a week, half of which was posted home to Auntie—came another season in Berlin. Bluebell came home to line up with The Jackson Girls in London, then went back to Europe—to Copenhagen, Barcelona, Budapest, and finally Paris—which she loved on sight with such intensity that she persuaded Jackson to let her stay there permanently. 'Auntie' found it a problem to grasp the essential purity of a life in which nudes now took their place, and spent several hours meticulously painting brassières on the girls pictured in the programmes her adopted daughter sent back to Liverpool.

The illusion that the life of a chorus girl is one of gaiety and pleasure unmitigated by any form of what could be called 'work' has by now been clearly despatched; and life with the Jacksons was certainly a sufficiently tough introduction to the business. Evasion of the tight discipline of the organisation was not easy even if one had the energy to try. The 'danger' of a romance was keener and more easily embraced within the theatre than outside it, and the boys in the band were among the most persistent of the girls' suitors. Miss Bluebell was wooed with great determination by the orchestra's pianist, Marcel Leibovici—who in 1939 was to capture and marry her. Soon, she found herself Captain of the Folies Jacksons, with an extra five shillings a week to prove it.

But then came the kind of blow not uncommon in show business. Paul Derval, the owner and manager of the Folies, announced that he could no longer afford the Jacksons; and the promptness with which he turned down the immediate offer from Jackson of a cut in the girls' salaries, suggested that he simply no longer wanted the troupe. Bluebell joined the Casino de Paris Jacksons—and then came a break which was really to set her on her way. Derval sent for her, told her that he had always admired her work, and asked her if she would be interested in forming her own troupe of girls for the Folies. She raced around contacting her friends, offering them work or seducing them from the work they were doing—and soon the first Bluebell Girls danced happily through a four-month season.

Derval was pleased, and told Bluebell that he would happily re-engage them for the next show, which was to star the great Mistinguett. But 'Miss' would of course have to see the girls at work, and approve them. As luck would have it, the Bluebells were so intent on rehearsing beneath the stage that on the very evening the star attended a performance, they missed their entrance, and chaos ensued. 'Miss' was understandably horrified, and the Bluebell Girls were out of work.

Again, it proved a blessing in disguise. Miss Bluebell was extremely interested in the work of the Buddy Bradley Girls, a new troupe who replaced the Bluebells. The Bradleys were all tall girls, and had broken away from the very simple kicking routine which was the rule with the Tillers and most other chorus-lines—they broke the line, and did 'tap'

Miss Bluebell (left) with the Jacksons in Munich, 1929, and (below) rehearsing at the Paris Lido, 1952

Overleaf: The cast of Camelot at the Theatre Royal, Drury Lane, in 1964, wore magnificent costumes designed by John Truscott, and the visual element of Robert Helpmann's production contributed greatly to its success. Ladies of the chorus only rarely in the past decade had such opportunities for displaying really ambitious costumes

and other numbers. Bluebell decided that she would take this even further. She too would concentrate on engaging tall girls—who always showed off to better advantage whatever costumes were designed for them—and she would give them more interesting work to do, work which would make it possible for them to develop their own personalities within the discipline of the troupe.

Meanwhile, she had eleven girls on her hands, for whom she felt responsible, and for whom she had no work. She trudged from theatre to theatre, agent to agent, and eventually ended up in the office of Jacques Charles, who was producing stage shows to punctuate the showing of films at the vast new Paramount Cinema in the Boulevard des Italiens. Yes, he would be glad of a troupe—but his stage was so big that a dozen girls would be lost on it. Could Bluebell provide a troupe of twenty-four?

'The Bluebell Girls' went up for the first time in lights at the front of a theatre: and soon Derval and Mistinguett were casting somewhat jealous eyes on the Paramount Cinema. There had been problems at the Folies. Could Bluebell provide a second troupe of girls for the next Folies revue? She could. She did. A second troupe of sixteen girls was formed—then another, to tour Italy—and still Bluebell herself was dancing with her Paramount troupe, and sitting up half the night in her hotel room after the show, working out the details of contracts, organising train-timetables . . . Rather sadly, she decided that she must be either a dancer or an impresario. The choice was obvious.

In 1935, Bluebell left Paris with the first touring troupe of her Girls, supporting an Italian comedian in a revue. It was her first visit to Italy, where troupes of Bluebells have continued to appear ever since. The name was getting known—by reputation only in England, where the Bluebells have only rarely appeared—and Miss Bluebell herself began to get letters requesting auditions. As the troupe became better-known, there was a wider and wider choice of girls, and her reputation for providing hard-working, experienced professionals who were also extremely beautiful, was established.

The war, of course, put paid to Bluebell's success for the time. The Paris troupe left for England, and the Italian troupe escaped by the skin of its teeth on one of the last trains to leave that country before she entered the war. Bluebell herself stayed in France, and was interned; her husband—half-Jewish—went into hiding. After six months, the Irish Ambassador in Paris managed to prove Bluebell's Dublin birth, and she was released. Marcel and she continued to meet, and he was eventually captured by the Gestapo—but managed to escape from the concentration camp to which he was sent.

Their meetings continued, and during the war Miss Bluebell had four children—which took some explaining to the Gestapo, who were always calling in attempts to recapture Marcel. It is to be feared that Miss Bluebell did nothing to allay the traditional doubts about the honour and decency of the chorus girl by her explanation: 'What do you expect a healthy girl to do when you take away her husband?'

At the end of the war, the indefatigable Miss Bluebell, now in her

Above: A line-up of Bluebell Girls poses in a garden in Morocco in 1936. Right: Some Bluebell show-girls at the Paris Lido; 1964

In 1972 an attempt to stage Gone With the Wind, the well-known novel and more famous film, as a musical was a relative failure: but the costume designs for principals and chorus were among the most beautiful seen recently at Drury Lane

Extrovert dancers from the Natal Theatre Workshop Zulu Company injected tribal dances from South Africa into Umabatha, a version of Macbeth (left). The production caused a sensation during the 1973 and 1974 World Theatre seasons in London. Equally far from the popular idea of a chorus-line is (below) the opera chorus, here seen as they appeared in the English National Opera Company's 1969 production of Gilbert and Sullivan's Patience, in John Stoddart's magnificent art nouveau costumes for the Twenty Love-sick Maidens

Two of Miss Bluebell's show-girls at the Paris Lido in the 1970s. The costume of the girl on the right might, with some modification, have been designed for an Edwardian chorus-girl

Overleaf: one of the patterns of girls with which, in his film of Sandy Wilson's The Boy Friend, Ken Russell paid tribute to the greatest director of musical films, Busby Berkeley

Bluebells at the Paramount
Cinema, Paris (see p. 118)

thirties, set about rebuilding her troupes. Within weeks of the liberation, the first reappeared at the Folies; and three years later, when M. Volterre opened the Lido in a vast underground cellar on the Champs Elysées, Les Bluebelles made their usual sensation, and have been doing so ever since.

The vast popularity of English girls in Paris and elsewhere rests on the keenness and expertise of the girls themselves, under expert direction. As to finding those girls—Peter Baker, Miss Bluebell's English manager, has for years been attending her auditions, and holding auditions of his own, seeing girls from Europe, Australia and New Zealand, South Africa . . . He has, as Miss Bluebell has, the sort of sixth sense cultivated by all the great impresarios from George Edwardes to Ziegfeld and Cochran, and which tells him instantly what a girl can do, just how she will make an effect. It is a sixth sense which is compacted of the other five, for he watches how a girl enters a room, how she walks, how she sits; he listens to what she has to say in response to careful questioning. Often, he doesn't even ask her to dance.

Audiences, he says, know nothing about dancing—and obviously this is, up to a point, true. The girls who go straight into the Bluebells

from the Royal Ballet School can certainly dance, and the fact that they are often out in front performing the more difficult features of the choreography for a scene, supports the fact that they are engaged for professionalism as well as for looks, personality, stamina and *oomph*. All of them must have a certain amount of professional dancing technique, simply in order that they can follow the instructions of the choreographer and producer. But there is much to be said for Miss Bluebell's invariable instruction: 'If you go wrong, go wrong smiling!' An audience will forgive a girl almost everything if she remains cool, smiling, attractive, unflustered.

It is interesting that it is basic ballet training which is important: a knowledge of 'modern dance' is not enough, though an instinct for movement in general, a certain flair, is necessary too. So is a beautiful body, and sheer sexiness, and the necessary height—over 5 ft. 7 in. A girl may protest if she is perfect in every respect but being only 5 ft. $6\frac{1}{2}$ in. tall. She is not rejected because of the half-inch, but because of the comparison the audience will be making not between her and the girl half-an-inch taller, but between her and the tallest girl in the troupe. The line has to be drawn somewhere.

It is a positive advantage for a ballet-trained girl who has grown taller than might have been expected, to know that a troupe like the Bluebells is in search of talent. The tall girl has traditionally been at an enormous disadvantage in classical ballet, partly because of the difficulty of finding a male partner who can cope with her. So the Royal Ballet School may advise a tall girl of sixteen or seventeen to audition for Miss Bluebell—not at all dismayed by the fact that the troupe includes girls who dance bare-breasted.

This would once no doubt have caused a mild sensation: but it is an everyday matter today. In any event, no girl *has* to dance topless (nor can she expect extra payment for doing so). It is entirely a voluntary matter, and the fact that there is never a shortage of girls happy to show off their bodies in a beautiful and appropriate setting seems to argue that the Royal Ballet School is right to take this as a matter of course.

Mr Baker, and Miss Bluebell herself, take great pains in grooming girls for the troupes, as well as in choosing already mature performers. This is a major secret of their success—and an index of that success is the fact that a Bluebell Girl's salary in Paris or Las Vegas is probably higher than a comparable salary paid to any other chorus girl in the world.

The size of the salary, no less than the prestige, attracts the great number of girls competing for a place in a Bluebell troupe. A girl the height of whose hopes in England might be a season at the Palladium for perhaps £34 a week, plus a fairly short summer season at £25 or £30, will obviously turn her eyes abroad where she can earn a salary which will keep her in comfort and enable her to save for her future.

A girl of fourteen may audition for the Bluebells, and if she obviously has a flair for the work, and looks like being a beauty, she will be carefully watched over the next year or so—a diet may be suggested, her weight will be checked, her bearing will be improved, and eventually, when she is sixteen or seventeen, she will be re-auditioned.

While a great deal of time is taken in selecting and grooming the girls, an equal amount of time is taken up by organisation: show business involves not only 'showing' but 'business'. Contracts are approved by the actors' union; and apart from the actual conditions of employment and salary, the Bluebell organisation patently pays enormous attention to its girls' well-being, carrying on the tradition of the theatre since George Edwardes' day by carefully arranging transport (often as far afield as Japan), accommodation, and other details.

It is difficult not to believe that being a Bluebell is, in the 1970s, something most girls interested in the lighter side of the theatre would set their sights on. Next to being a star, what better than to be one of an immensely admired troupe, for whom the most glamorous and often expensive costumes are provided, whose routines are often extremely well choreographed and produced, and whose glamour is unassailable? The work is arduous, conditions backstage can still be far from ideal ideal (though much better in Las Vegas, say, than in all but the most modern English theatre). But if being a chorus girl means being a Bluebell, there is obviously much to be said for it.

Opposite above: The mystique of Hollywood retains its fascination, and at the Talk of the Town restaurant-cabaret (once the London Hippodrome, built to house a circus) a spectacular revue number recaptures the days of the all-singing, all-dancing, all-talking movie of the 1920s.

Below: Bluebell Girls at the Lido. With total nudity breaking through in revue and drama, the chorus- and show-girls of Paris tend now to rely for their best effects on gay, extrovert costumes.

'Five minutes, please!'

A typical audition line in the 1930s, the girl in the middle in her underclothes (above).
Right: A visitor back-stage in about 1885

Top: Backstage at the Folies
Bergère—in London, on tour, in
1949. Left: Girls on tour find a
boarding-house (1947)

131

Above: The costume fitting-
room at the Windmill, 1951.
Right: 'Irene' and 'Terry' in
a dressing-room at the Paris
Folies

132

Above: A sandwich in the dressing-room at the Place Pigalle, Piccadilly (1951), where the girls were all English. Below: an unoccupied costume, woman-handled to the wardrobe. Right: a Windmill Girl between shows

'It hurts me to confess it, but I'd have given ten conversations with

Einstein for a first meeting with a pretty chorus girl.' Albert Camus

If the chorus enjoyed special attention in the 1920s, it was for a very obvious reason: men who had endured years in the mud of the Flanders trenches were not attracted to the more serious plays in the West End. They walked out of *Ghosts*, talked through *The Cherry Orchard*; they flocked to the Comedy to see Owen Nares in *The Charm School*, and to the Criterion for Cyril Maude, newly returned from New York to play in *Lord Richard in the Pantry*. And, above all, they demanded musical comedy and revue, with rows of deliciously leggy chorus girls in unlikely costumes and situations.

There was no shortage of musicals: at the Adelphi, *The Naughty Princess*; on the vast stage of the Theatre Royal, Drury Lane, *The Garden of Allah*; at the bottom of the Haymarket, *Chu Chin Chow* still pulling in packed houses towards the end of a run that was to remain a British theatre record until *The Mousetrap*, fifty years later. But smaller shows also did well: *A Little Dutch Girl* at the Lyric, for instance, and *Bran Pie* at the Prince of Wales. And there was always variety at the London Palladium or the Victoria Palace . . .

Theatre managers and backers recognised the new mood, born of a desperation to forget the horrors of the past five years. More and more theatres allowed smoking, and even women now smoked in public. Evening dress began to vanish from the stalls and circle, except on first nights. The audiences were relatively easily pleased: elderly ladies and gentlemen who had never set eyes on a chorus girl before (or at least, only clandestinely) now gazed bemusedly up through a haze of cigarette smoke at the rows of dancing girls—though there were limits; Queen Mary was ostentatiously to avert her eyes from a stage filled, unprecedentedly, with girls in bathing costumes, during a visit to *No, No, Nanette*.

There was still plenty of work about for a chorus girl—and not only in the West End, where the average musical might have a chorus of 100 or 150 girls. This could not rival the great old days when George Edwardes supported a chorus of 200 girls at the Empire—but most London musicals, if they were successful, sent out at least one or two touring companies to the provinces, often before the original version had ended its West End run. These trailed around from town to town, show-trains dragging the cast from one dreary lodginghouse to the next. A chain of theatrical boarding-houses was built up, their landladies, often legendary monsters, specialising in caring for theatre people—providing late meals after late curtains, not turning the girls out of bed too early in the morning, and gritting their teeth to the smell of kippers frying over a spirit-stove in the bedroom (for salaries were often minute). *The Maid of the Mountains* thus supported (after a fashion) fourteen provincial companies at one time, employing at least 600 girls —and, of course, some boys.

The chorus boy plays no prominent part in this book: and his part in show-business as a whole is slender, though it could scarcely have done without him. He has always been a somewhat androgynous figure: often unfairly so, no doubt. Mae West, running her own show on Broadway, once told an interviewer:

Previous pages: **The chorus of** Sunny **at the London Hippodrome, 1926—one of the most popular shows of its decade**

'I'm having a nice, easy time for a change. You see, a musical show usually has a lot of girls, and they're as troublesome as a cage-full of monkeys. Always fightin' an' up to mischief. But in this show I use a chorus of boys. They're sittin' right now in their dressin'-rooms, drinking their hot milk, an' doin' their knittin' as good as gold.'

There have always been plenty of heterosexual chorus-boys; but it has equally always been true that some managements have positively welcomed the homosexual, as being a greater perfectionist, more happily intent on keeping a costume in perfect order, willing and able to sew on a button or mend a seam, and paying vast attention to detail in performance. One doubts whether this is much more true of the homosexual than the heterosexual dancer; and if the girls in a company are marginally less likely to have their bottoms pinched on the way to the dressing-room, this may not be entirely welcome on a long and boring tour.

In the 1920s, apart from touring shows, a few girls were fortunate enough to secure permanent contracts. At the Victoria Palace, for instance—a variety theatre—the Victoria Girls so delighted patrons that the programmes were able to announce: 'Owing to the continued popularity of their delightful dancers, the Directors have renewed their contract for a further lengthy period.' This was as near to total security as any chorus girl could expect to get.

Opposite: An Erté design for the boys of the chorus at the Casino de Paris, 1971. Below: The boys' dressing-room at the Adelphi in 1930: the show was Evergreen

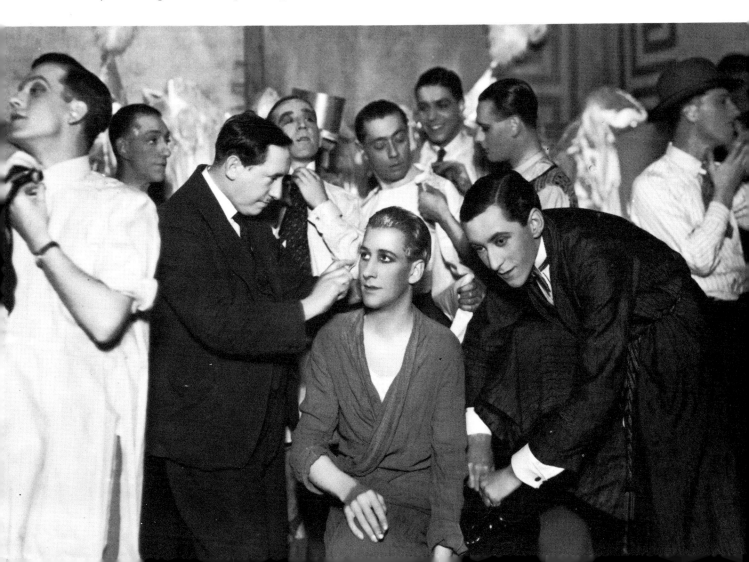

Opposite, above: The Dancing Belles in That's a Good Girl! at the London Hippodrome, 1928. Below: The Victoria Girls, in 1927 (see p. 137)

However strenuous the work, there was keen competition for it. Husbands and fathers killed in the war had left many young women without men to support them, and auditions were often distressing experiences, as hundreds of girls beseeched impresarios for work. One manager remembered them for the rest of his life:

'Fifty candidates for the chorus, each of them gripping a sheet of music, stretched in a long line from the wings up the long stairs to the street, all patiently waiting to sing a few bars of a much-rehearsed song. First would come a dainty weak-voiced maiden aged thirteen, sent by a doting mother from a distant provincial town to become a chorus-girl. Next one who in her fright started to climb upon her chair in the middle of the stage when bidden to stand near it. Then an elderly woman who on being turned down begged for a chance to "do anything, even clean the floors," only "something to do to earn a living . . ."

In a deplorable plight, one disappointed candidate asked for the loan of a shilling for a meal before leaving. Strong, even beautiful and moving voices sometimes filled the dark theatre, but the music master shook his head. The good clothes of the candidates, which they did not wear with ease, their awkward gait, their self-conscious faces, told against them . . .'

Many of the girls lacked the money to provide themselves with reasonable clothes. It was all very well for C. B. Cochran to complain that girls often turned up at auditions with dirty clothes and untidy hair: the poor creatures, often enough, had no choice. Undoubtedly many of them were sufficiently desperate to grasp any means of persuading a manager to employ them, and if the casting couch played any serious part in the theatre tradition, it was during this period. There is not a great deal of evidence to show that it did; but managers and impresarios being human and susceptible as any other man, and being surrounded from day to day by beautiful girls anxious to get on in the theatre, one may draw one's own conclusions.

There were many men whose kind hearts provided girls with regular employment years after their meagre talents had died under the weight of increasing age and *avoirdupois*. Ivor Novello, for instance, could never bear to reject any girl he had employed in previous shows. Right to the end of his life, at auditions, he would groan as some plump, middle-aged lady walked on-stage who he remembered from his earliest musicals. 'I really *can't* employ all these old ducks,' he would tell his stage manager; 'not again!' But on opening night, there the old girls would be, in the back row of the singing chorus, mouthing the lyrics of the songs they could not really sing—virtually part of a private pension scheme.

During this period, C. B. Cochran's Young Ladies were, for England, the equivalent of Ziegfeld's Girls. 'Uniformly young and ladylike,' James Agate said, they were carefully selected by Cochran to decorate his revues. They were there, of course, to titillate and delight; but they did so with the utmost discretion, sometimes just posing in a row, sometimes cast as debutantes or sailors or 'a barracks of adorably simpering infantrymen', as in *Follow the Sun*.

The Young Ladies were an *élite*—chorus girls on the way to becoming show girls or stars (as many of them did: Florence Desmond, Anna Neagle, Jessie Matthews . . .). Each one was watched and nurtured, and on £8 to £10 a week considered herself fortunate. Sometimes she did an individual number in the course of a revue, and off-stage she was a minor celebrity in her own right.

Cochran was an adept publicist, and at a time when curves were beginning to become once more a part of the female figure, in 1929, he called in a dietetic specialist, Sir William Armstrong, to view the chorus of *Wake up and Dream* at the Pavilion—whose average weight was 8 stone 4 pounds (115 lb). 'What', asked Cochran, as publicly as possible, 'can I do about this state of affairs?' 'Chocolates,' replied the sensible Sir William, and Cochran presented each girl with a weekly box of chocolates, and also drew up with his dietician menus largely consisting of cream, peas, fresh milk, butter and wholemeal bread, in order to produce a larger girl with a proper distribution of female flesh. This campaign for plumper chorus girls got Cochran maximum publicity at the time, and seems not to have resulted in any diminution of his male audiences.

As always, the Young Ladies collected admirers. Sometimes, men focussed on an individual girl (presumably rightly assuming that a star would consider them beneath notice), and made a determined set at her —sending her flowers, hanging around the stage-door, and making endless nuisances of themselves. One girl remembered what it was like to be one of the prettier members of a chorus:

Above: Outside the stage-door of the Palace Theatre, London, girls gather for an audition for Mr Cochrane's Young Ladies. Below: The Young Ladies at the London Pavilion in 1930, in a 'Venetian Theatre' scene

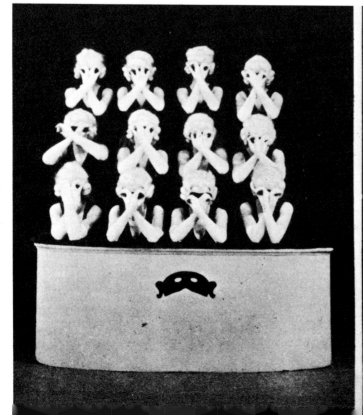

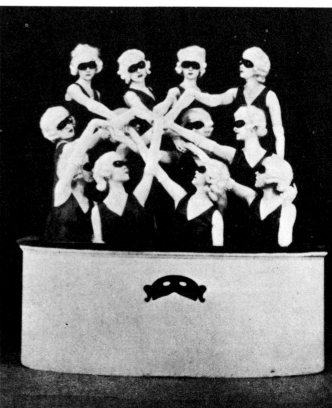

'I got numbers of all sorts of letters from men, saying all sorts of silly things; but then, there is nothing unique about that. That is simply one of the penalties of being a chorus girl. Every girl on the stage receives these kind of letters. It would seem that the fizzle of the spotlight on the actress has the power of fizzling up the hearts of susceptible menfolk. Of course the letters are not all silly, but there are some people who write really as if they were lunatics. There was one man who used to write to me every day, for I am sure almost half a year. He always used to sign himself "Your humble and trembling footlight." I'm sure he was a lunatic.'

In general, unless he had particular charm or determination, a young man had to be either very well-connected or extremely rich to have a chance of luring one of the chorus out to dinner—let alone the complete chorus; but occasionally there were evenings which developed into something as near an orgy as any respectable girl might expect. W. MacQueen Pope recalled one party given in an hotel after the first night of a not very promising musical, *The Little Girl in Red*, at the Gaiety in 1921:

'There were lots of celebrities, and the champagne flowed like water. Everybody made speeches, some clear, some incoherent. One girl began to speak, and then after a few words said "Oh golly, I feel Uncle Dick!" [rhyming Cockney slang: 'Uncle Dick'—sick] She was hurried from the room. In the small hours, two of the girls in the chorus who disliked each other had a fresh quarrel and fought it out with chairs . . .'

On-stage, the girls had to be prepared to shed some of the lady-like propriety which they were encouraged to maintain on the public side of the stage-door. Though stage nudity was impossible in the 1920s, there were scenes of decadence quite sufficient to attract the attention of puritans, and at the same time (and for the same reasons) overflowing audiences. After the enormous success of *Chu Chin Chow*, Oscar Ashe produced a spectacular musical at His Majesty's entitled *Cairo*, in which there was a scene which became notorious overnight: it took place in an old ruined Egyptian palace, where the villain gave a party, saying that it was 'probably a place where Cleopatra and her countless lovers, ages ago, did carouse, disport and sin.' A first-nighter described the scene:

'A line of flickering, flaming braziers competed
with the moonlight which drenched the scene. All was
silence. Then a perfect tidal wave of humanity, half-
naked, howling, singing, laughing and shouting, broke
over the stage. The brass blared, cymbals crashed,
and drums thundered, and throbbed, as that mob went
seemingly crazy. Everything was bizarre, fantastic,
utterly uninhibited. Women who seemed almost nude were
lifted aloft on the shoulders of men, to be dragged
down and embraced in abandoned attitudes by other men.
Girls like furies with flowing hair of green, red
and all other hues threw themselves on the villain,
who sat enthroned like a prince, smothered him with
lascivious gestures, and fought for his favour. It
was wildly virile, a very whirlpool of colour, noise
and ceaseless movement. When the orgy was at its
height, the curtain fell so suddenly that it took the
audience by surprise. Then almost immediately it rose
again on a picture which left them breathless. The
noise, the movement and the music had gone. There
was silence. The crowd of revellers worn out with
excess were strewn about in heaps everywhere, utterly
exhausted, a human débris, massed, conglomerate, their
white limbs gleaming in the moonlight and the torches'
glow. The festival of Saturn in ancient Rome could not
have been more ravishing to the eye.'

Decameron Nights at Drury Lane in 1922 had another scene which worried the censor, but was eventually passed:

'There was quite a sensation in a scene which showed
some monks rescuing apparently nude women from the sea,
while the waves roared, dashed over rocks and burst
into spray around them.'

The orgy scene from Cairo, 'A Mosaic in Music and Mime', at His Majesty's in 1921. It ran for 267 performances

THE FINALE, ACT II.

Warm in the all-embracing comfort of a flesh-coloured body-stocking, the 'apparently nude' young ladies, like their 'almost nude' sisters in Egypt, were still chorus girls. Indeed, it may have taken them almost as much courage and nerve to throw themselves enthusiastically into the brown, made-up arms of their chorus-boy slave lovers as it did for the cast of *The Dirtiest Show in Town*, half a century later, to reveal all in the cause of entertainment. More: for even apparent nudity, in the 1920s, was not only embarrassing but positively dangerous. It was not necessary for there to be physical contact between the girls and the men in their audience for a theatre manager to be convicted of keeping a disorderly house!

The 'real' nudes who were such a famous feature of The Windmill Theatre in London during the next three decades were not perhaps, strictly speaking, chorus girls: they neither sang nor danced. But they came of a long tradition of entertaining exhibitionism, stretching back to the eighteenth century and the more or less lacivious *anatomie vivante* exhibitions at which nude or semi-nude ladies posed for the

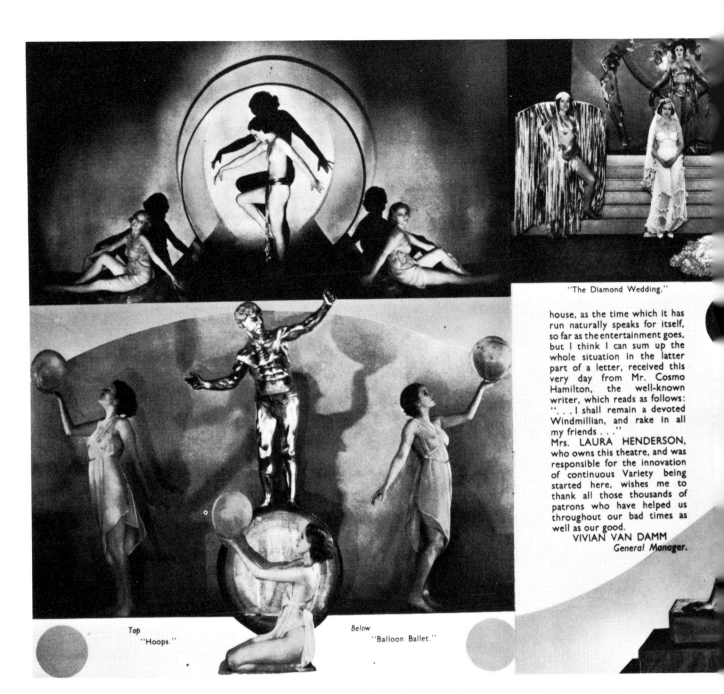

"The Diamond Wedding."

house, as the time which it has run naturally speaks for itself, so far as the entertainment goes, but I think I can sum up the whole situation in the latter part of a letter, received this very day from Mr. Cosmo Hamilton, the well-known writer, which reads as follows: "... I shall remain a devoted Windmillian, and rake in all my friends ..."
Mrs. LAURA HENDERSON, who owns this theatre, and was responsible for the innovation of continuous Variety being started here, wishes me to thank all those thousands of patrons who have helped us throughout our bad times as well as our good.
VIVIAN VAN DAMM
General Manager.

Top
"Hoops."

Below
"Balloon Ballet."

delight of gentlemen allegedly studying anatomy (the equivalent of the 'photographers' who pay considerable sums for the provision of a studio and nude models, but only rarely bother to load their cameras).

The Windmill was—is, for it has now re-opened as a theatre after some years as a cinema—a tiny theatre seating only just over 300 people, tucked away in a back street near Piccadilly. Vivian van Damm started *Revuedeville* there in 1932, concentrating on providing a revue which ran non-stop from 12.15 am until 10.35 pm every day except Sunday, with comedians doing their best to fill in the few minutes between the scenes in which conventional chorus girls danced, but in which seated nudes (strictly enjoined not to move so much as a finger, in order to comply with the censorship laws of the period) were the main attraction. There were peripheral pleasures, too: fan-dancers, for instance, and girls naked beneath diaphanous veils or gowns—though some insisted on wearing rather obvious panties, for additional protection.

The theatre attracted what has been called 'the dirty mackintosh

"The Vine."

Pages from an illustrated programme sold at the Windmill in 1934, two years after 'revuedeville' had started there

brigade', from their habit of sitting in the front rows (sometimes climbing over the seats, in the intervals, to get there!) with mackintoshes draped over their knees. A man was regularly placed in the wings to watch the audience, and would descend to remove any gentlemen whose restlessness reached disturbing proportions.

But however near the wind Mr van Damm managed to steer, conditions of work at the Windmill, if strenuous, were really rather good. Over 70 girls, some of them only fifteen, played in three productions which ran for six weeks each. The alternating casts each took the fourth show off, had a couple of weeks' holiday, and spent the other four weeks rehearsing the next production. The girls (who by 1952 were getting £10 a week) often went on to become stars in their own right, as did the comedians who had to work against the strong opposition of the nudes the gentlemen had really come to see.

It is notable that everyone was proud to work, or have worked, at the Windmill: it became a tradition of its own, and few girls are ashamed to announce that they took part in shows there. There is a strong contrast with the totally nude shows of the 1970s, photographs of which are sometimes unobtainable because actors or actresses who appeared in them seem ashamed to have it known that they removed their clothes in public.

Seemingly so 'naughty' in its day, the Windmill would now seem cosy indeed. But in its own time, it was a legend, and especially so during the Second World War, when the girls occasionally left the Windmill to give shows for the troops in large and draughty aircraft hangars. On one celebrated occasion, Mr van Damm arranged a special production number in which the girls, clad in leotards, danced under ultra-violet lighting which made them appear naked. Alas, the men in the audience, dissatisfied with the lighting arrangements, produced their torches and shone them at the stage—revealing, of course, costumes rather than skin.

'We Never Closed' became the motto of the Windmill, which ran throughout the war—providing on one occasion a spectacularly memorable moment when a bomb dropped near the theatre, and ever so slowly the motionless nude at the centre of a tableau lifted an arm to thumb her nose at the sky; the one recorded occasion when a Windmill nude actually moved.

More alarming—for some—than nudity or suggestiveness was the religiosity which followed Cochran's wildly successful production of *The Miracle* at Olympia in 1911, and which prompted other less talented managers to inject a note of piety into the most unlikely productions. In the middle of *Palladium Pleasures*, in 1926, for example, there was a ballet danced by Diaghilev's discovery, Anton Dolin, in which a Miss Toots Pound was snatched momentarily from the chorus into stardom to appear as the Virgin Mary; and there have been some singularly awful 'ballets' in which nuns have been reduced to near-nakedness by prancing devils.

But such absurdities were only part of the fun of the musical theatre of the 1920s and 1930s. A girl engaged for chorus work never quite knew what she might be doing next—from a *religioso* number in one revue to one choreographed by Balanchine in another; or, dashing off-stage after a dance-number in a musical, she would run panting up the iron stairs to her dressing-room, and there—elbowing off her colleagues as best she might—hasten into breeches to appear as one of a crowd of jockeys, or into a well-fitting uniform, as a guardsman. The delight, for the audience, was partly in the very absurdity of the goings-on. James Agate, in his notice of *The New Moon,* recalled the moment when, on a ship in the gulf of Mexico, the crew

'were presently joined by a number of female pirates as prettily garbed as attendants at a picture palace. After which . . . we were landed on an island beach and admired the handsome way in which the lady-sailors transformed themselves into Mexican beauties and enlivened the local mango-swamps with white organdie and dancing pumps.'

But a dangerously exciting note was entering the theatre at the same time: in 1921, Mae Murray and a chorus-line introduced into a New York show that new, modern, advanced, degenerate dance the *shimmy.* The turning-in of the toes and knees, followed by the *frisson,* or sexy wiggle of the bottom, 'was thought by some to be vulgar,' said *The Times,* going on to quote the Archbishop of Canterbury (who had not at that time actually seen the dance) as saying that the *shimmy* 'may be harmless, but the manner of dancing it is degenerate.'

Chorus girls were warned by 'a Harley Street specialist' that 'girls who sacrifice their nerves and beauty to the *shimmy* will be claimed by old age.' They were no doubt already sufficiently aware of the shortness of their careers. But the *shimmy* never really took on in England; the even more sensational Black Bottom did—and so did the ubiquitous Charleston.

The Charleston had originally been a Negro round dance; discovered in 1923 among the black dock-workers in Charleston, South Carolina, it had been taken to New York and used to provide a set-piece in the Ziegfeld Follies at the New Amsterdam Theatre, and then toured America as part of a revue with a black chorus, *Runnin' Wild.*

In England, audiences crowded the Palladium in 1926 to see *Blackbirds,* a revue in which the black chorus stunned the fans to whom the Tillers had previously represented the polite epitome of dash and vigour. 'Such attack, such speed and such complete team-work, and so much talent packed into one show has seldom been witnessed,' one critic wrote; and James Agate, never easy to please at revue, at least had 'never seen dancing to compete with that given by these Black Birds.'

Of course there was a strong element of sexuality both in the dancing and the girls themselves, and some critics shrank from it, shrilly complaining that the Blackbirds were 'freakish', 'degenerate', and 'negroid'. *The Daily Mail* found the entire chorus indulging in 'a series of contortions without a vestige of grace or charm, reminiscent only of

THE BLACKBIRDS.

Lew Leslie's " BLACKBIRDS OF 1934," at the London Coliseum, are a company of brilliant and versatile artists. The top left-hand photograph on this page shows VALAIDA, the star, with NYAS BERRY, whose numbers include the popular " Papa de Da Da." The other photographs are studies of the BLACKBIRDS BEAUTY CHORUS, who are full of vitality, swagger, and style.

A publicity photograph of some of the Blackbirds taken on the roof of the London Pavilion, where British audiences saw them for the first time in 1926

negro orgies.' The Rev. E. W. Rogers, Vicar of St Aldin's, Bristol warned that 'Any lover of the beautiful will die rather than be associated with it . . . It is neurotic! It is rotten! It stinks!' His senior colleague the Bishop of Coventry found the Black Bottom 'a very nice dance', however, and audiences who crowded the Palladium at every performance put their approbation even more enthusiastically.

Charleston—Black Bottom—Varsity Drag: these were all introduced to England by the ladies of the chorus, though they were taken up in the dance-halls by pullulating amateurs. The girls' repertoire of dance-steps was growing: now they had to be adept at every modern dance, as well as ballet, tap and perhaps acrobatics; and if they could manage to cultivate reasonable singing voices, so that they could pant out a song during a routine, so much the better. They also had to be able to act—if only occasionally. In *Merely Molly*, as early as 1926, the first act had been set in London's east end, and a chorus of girls appeared not in glamorous gowns but in imitation silk stockings with authentic cotton tops and trade-marks, quite unlike the costumes of the pretty girls who disported themselves on the beach in *Lido Lady* or *The Blue Train*, or provided the conventional chorus of mindless beautiful blondes in *Oh, Kay!* In 1927, in *Show Boat*, the curtains went up to show—instead of the obligatory row of girls belting out some mindless number—a gang of black dock workers complaining about the heaviness of the cotton bales they had to hump; and when the girls of the town arrived on the arms of their *beaux*, the show's first number, *Cotton Blossom*, had as a counterpoint the negroes' painful complaint.

But these exceptions were against the grain: *White Horse Inn*, even the universally popular Ivor Novello musicals, continued to use the

chorus much as before; and the war did nothing to change things in England—people went to the theatre to get away from the blitz or the deadening horror of the daily headlines. It was no time for social realism —certainly not in the musical theatre.

The chorus's contribution to the war effort was less apparent than the stars'—many of the latter joined ENSA, the national organisation which sent show-people abroad to entertain the troops. Simply because it was never very easy to transport more than a few people through war-torn Europe, not many ENSA shows had choruses, and many of the beautiful girls who had delighted West End audiences before the war disappeared into the forces, or into factory work.

But there were one or two notable exceptions: like Mrs Cyril Barker's Concert Party, run by the indefatigable Gabrielle Barker, who got together a chorus of nine girls who often performed as many as twenty dance numbers on shaky improvised stages in the desert, in and out of tents, on the backs of lorries, on Royal Navy ships—even at one time in the impressive Cairo Opera House—throughout the Middle East.

On one military pass issued to the party in Egypt, where most of its performances were given, an official wrote: 'Object of visit—Giving Pleasure to the Troops.' Certainly the girls did that, sometimes incidentally, as when an ambitious soldier cut a slit in the dressing-room tent and stole a number of *brassières* which were later disposed of to willing bidders. On other occasions, men would fish for panties as they hung out to dry in the desert air. But the girls were not known as 'cast-iron virgins' for nothing; discipline was strict, and the entertainment provided was strictly choreographic.

A glamorous group in the revue After Dark at the Vaudeville Theatre in 1933

The chorus-line was never really reconstituted in its pre-war style. Even in 1939, it was usually cast in its old vein—and all the efforts of the Tillers, Miss Bluebell—even Balanchine—had failed to lift it out of the totally frivolous role in which it had been firmly cast by book- and libretto-writers. Most musicals still opened with the boys and girls gathered in front of a pasteboardy set, giving out with the sing-and-dance. In 1904, the curtain went up on *The Red Mill*, to discover a band of beautiful girls:

'By the side of the mill with its quaint sails
    hanging still and the bridge so quaint,
We've been posing for hours with our baskets of
    flowers as they paint, paint, paint . . .'

And the boys, artists to a man, carefully ignored their models' intoxicating proximity to reply:

'Girls, as you know we are wed alone to art
    And it breaks our heart
But we have to devote all our own to art . . .'

Twenty years later, at the beginning of *No, No, Nanette*, Pauline, James Smith's maid, opened the door to a collection of choristers who announced themselves:

'Flappers are we,
Flippant and fly and free,
Never too slow,
All on the go,
Petting parties with the smarties,
Moonlight dances,
Oh, what chances,
Keeping our beaux
Up on their toes,
Dizzy with dangerous glee . . .'

And throughout the show the chorus would return, balancing on beach-balls, dressed for a party, undressed for a dormitory scene, but essentially always the background against which the principals acted and sang out their love story.

Most English theatre people had their minds elsewhere, in 1943, than on the development of the musical comedy. Otherwise more notice would have been taken of a production which appeared on Broadway in April of that year, which within a few years was to have demolished tradition, and finished off the old-fashioned musical for ever (except as a piece of nostalgic reconstruction). It was *Oklahoma!* As Jack Burton, the American critic, put it:

'This phenomenal production sets a new pattern
for girl-and-music shows in which every line, every
song, every dance routine is an indispensable part of
a closely-knit whole.'

It was the beginning of the great era of American musicals, with *Annie Get Your Gun* opening shortly afterwards to consolidate the success. The old-style musical hung on for a while (*Brigadoon*, in 1947, still had a chorus of 'merry villagers'), but soon, in London as well as on Broadway, the chorus became part of the story of a show—the boys and girls were now (more or less, according to talent) also actors, with their individual rôles to play. They sang, they danced—but *Oklahoma!* had had choreography by Agnes de Mille which demanded a great deal from them, and the musical director, Jack Blackton, had made vocal arrangements in multiple parts. There were sixteen singers who could also dance, and eighteen dancers who could also sing. Nothing could have been further from the posing Girls of George Edwardes or Flo Ziegfeld.

The increased reality of the musical contributed too to a changing style of production: the Romeo-and-Juliet plot of *West Side Story* did not allow for 'pretty' sets or costumes, and indeed ultimate reality was reached when that show was filmed actually in the streets of New York.

The change had one important financial aspect: a chorus boy or girl expected to sing moderately difficult music and to dance often very difficult choreography, was no longer content with a small salary; but increased salaries, especially towards the end of the 1960s, placed such an additional burden on producers that choruses shrank and eventually all but disappeared. Good dancers, especially, have always been rare, and can command larger salaries than singers. A show which is to look half-way reasonable on a large stage can scarcely get away with fewer than sixteen dancers, and a minimal chorus now costs so much that a producer will only gamble on a show of which he is completely confident. And confidence, in the theatre, comes hard.

So, the theatre of the 1970s only rarely employs large choruses: the revival of *No, No, Nanette* which delighted Broadway in 1971 was an exception—supervised by Busby Berkeley, it had a large chorus, and its producers were cruelly particular in their supervision of its com-

Above: On-stage rehearsal for Show Boat **at Drury Lane (1928).** Below: Sophistication was the keynote of Noël Coward's Words and Music **at the Adelphi (1932)**

Opposite, above: A mildly salacious scene **from** These Foolish Things **at the Palladium (1938). Below: Chorus girls in cabaret at London's Piccadilly Hotel (1929)**

position. But that show cost $600,000 to mount (though it made a profit of $25,000 a week after six months in New York). When it opened in London, economies were made in the chorus, with the result that the splendour of a scene in which 60 boys all playing ukeleles to the chorus of *Tea for Two* was reduced to the apparent dimensions of a village hall pantomime, on the vast Drury Lane stage. The show did not run in England, and although indifferent casting contributed, the lack of a really splendid chorus was a main ingredient of the failure.

But in the present financial situation, with escalating production costs, the chorus has largely left the modern musical.

A Grecian Idyll

They never moved

Above: While the solitary nude hardly dares breathe, her friend in flowers and a boy in a none-too-secure beach-towel have a ball at the Windmill, c. 1938.
Right: See-through demi-semi-blouses at the Windmill.
Opposite, above: One of the famous fan dances and (below) hard work in rehearsal

'Giving pleasure to the troops'

Left: A brave Windmill Girl
offers her All from a makeshift
stage in a theatre of war. Right:
Autographs after the show.
Below, left and centre: ENSA
girls in the Middle East. Below,
right: Packing the costumes

8 The Chorus on Film

The power of the chorus being what it was, ranks of pretty girls found their way into films almost as soon as films found their way into projectors; and since they almost immediately began to dance, the provision of a soundtrack for them to dance to was important. In fact, sound for film (though not sound *on* film) was developed almost as early as the motion picture itself, and at the Paris Exposition of 1900 short films were shown in which Sarah Bernhardt spoke and Vesta Tilley sang.

As far as one can discover, it was Warner Brothers who presented the first team of dancers on sound film—that is, with the music coming from behind the cinema screen rather than from a pianist or orchestra in front of it: this was in August 1926, when the Cansinos (a Spanish dancing troupe) took part in a programme with Mischa Elman, Giovanni Martinelli and others. *Cinema Art* was astounded at the 'perfection' with which the music and dance steps matched: 'It was difficult to believe that they were not actually in front of the audience,' the critic enthused.

The coming of 'the talkies' proper—the recording of a sound-track on the film itself, obviating the necessity of synchronising a gramophone record with the film—created various problems, among them the sensitivity of the microphones, which recorded not only the dialogue, but the sound of heavy boots on the studio floor, the nervous breathing of the hero and heroine, the magnified sound of a kiss—not always as attractive as the sight! For a chorus, the problems were even greater. The girls in the strange, spangled bathing-costumes of *Lights of New York* (the first all-talking musical, made in 1928) or *Gold Diggers of Broadway* (the first of a long series, made the following year) found that a tap-dance number was virtually impossible: the noise was so deafening. Even the studio fans had to be turned off in case they interfered with the dialogue, and everyone tip-toed about in soft shoes. Old stagers were reminded of a song from an old 1910 musical, *The Spring Maid*:

'Clip-clop-clop,
Clip-clop-clop,
Over the tiles—
    Her feet
    were petite,
But you heard her for miles!'

The passion for '100% Talking 100% Singing 100% Dancing' films was so great in the early days, that many deals were made for the filming of stage successes before anyone had properly considered the problems. Ziegfeld signed a contract with Sam Goldwyn for the filming of *Whoopee*, then had to re-train all the cast, so that they could dance *quietly*, would remember not to open their mouths anywhere near a microphone . . . When *Rio Rita* was filmed, with its coronation scene in which girls with ostrich-feather fans lined the steps to the throne, the fans themselves had to be specially redesigned, because the originals

'Sam Goldwyn asked me what my first step would be, and I told him "Girls!"'

Busby Berkeley

Previous pages: Willard Mack surveys a line-up of girls before shooting a musical number for Ring up the Curtain (1933)

Opposite: Three of the Mack Sennet Bathing Beauties, 1918, to some degree echoing the proportions of the Gaiety Girls

161

162

clattered and creaked so much that the dialogue could not be heard.

Carpets were laid in the studios, and heavy drapes hung, for the convenience of the sound men; then it was found that the sight of a large chorus dancing without a sound from their feet was ridiculous. The orchestra was bustled from one corner of the studio to another, to get the balance right, before the idea of pre-recording the musical numbers, and dancing to the recordings, became a commonplace (which was surprisingly early: in *Hollywood Revue of 1929*, for instance).

When colour came in, the difficulties multiplied: in early colour films, or films with colour sequences, it was found that the colours in certain costumes looked horrific, and the stage designs had to be modified for film.

Gradually, the difficulties were ironed out, and the way was open for the chorus to take its proper place in film. Almost as soon as directors realised the additional possibilities of the medium, they began experimenting by using the chorus as though it were a sort of living kaleido-

Opposite, above: The girl passengers in an early moon-rocket which featured in the first science fiction film, Voyage dans la Lune **(1902). The director was George Meliés**

Below, left: Venus with her galley slaves, from the finale of Busby Berkeley's Fashions of 1934, in which the girls seemed clad only in ostrich feathers

Below, right: Nine Sennet girls afloat for a publicity picture. (Note the ubiquitous ukelele)

scope: in *Hollywood Revue*, for instance, the *Albertina Rasch Ballet Company* (a dignified title for what was just another chorus) was filmed by a camera slung over the dancers' heads, and the director arranged them to make flower-like patterns, in a pale foretaste of the Busby Berkeley patterns to come. In the finale, the girls, in green tutus against a green background (and so more or less invisible!) performed a demi-semi-ballet before hastily changing into transparent raincoats and hats for the earliest version of *Singin' in the Rain*, accompanied by Ukelele Ike (one of the earliest clips in the recent retrospective of musical films, *That's Entertainment*).

Some of the sequences in early musical films make one wonder about the standards of chorus-dancing in the stage musicals of the period: girls were ill-matched, tapping and kicking with more vigour and enthusiasm than unanimity; arms were badly placed, looking as though they were all elbows and wrists; pointe work, when it occurred, was enthusiastic but lax; there were bent knees, misplaced hips, sickled feet; and a 'shoulder leg' (in which a girl gripping her lower leg, hopped on the other foot) was embarrassing with the legs all at various altitudes and angles.

One great advantage of the film was, of course, the possibility of spectacular settings which could not possibly have been built on conventional theatre stages. Sometimes the camera, too, soared high above the chorus, giving the audience a bird's-eye view never possible in the theatre, and covering a scene of enormous complexity and often great beauty, in which much depended on the girls being draped around the right bits of set at the right time. Visual scenes were orchestrated with the greatest care, and while often all that was required of the chorus was that the girls should lie still and look beautiful, they often had to do this for hours on end, perhaps clutching a harp or 'playing' a piano, and supporting a costume as heavily uncomfortable as it was spectacular.

No wonder Busby Berkeley told an interviewer years later that 'you had to look for more than pretty faces and shapely limbs. The girls needed intelligence, co-ordination, and the ability to understand intricate routines—plus endurance, since the work was long and tiring.' One has only to see such a scene as the staircase number in *The Great Zeigfeld* to appreciate the difficulties; many such scenes have never been out-done.

If it was possible, now, for a director to use girls as wallpaper or carpeting, it was also possible for him to bring an individual member of the audience into close contact with each individual member of the chorus: the camera learned to linger lovingly a foot or two away, before moving on to the next beauty; and one or other of them would have their effect.

The picture of the film chorus girl as a wild and wicked woman may, in the early 1920s, have been somewhat justified. There was enormous competition (by 1920, 14,354 women were listed professionally as 'screen actresses' in America), and as early as 1914, *Variety* reported that 'in one New York studio it is asserted that no woman can work in

Previous pages: Willard Mack
consults a co-producer before
shooting one of the most
elaborate scenes in Ring up the
Curtain (1933)

Robert Z. Leonard mounted this
most spectacular of all scenes to
set off the song A Pretty Girl is
like a Melody in his The Great
Ziegfeld (1936)

that particular place unless countenancing the advances of "the boss", who has nothing to recommend himself for female fancy excepting an official position.'

No doubt many girls who hoped eventually to attain the position of Mary Pickford (who was earning $500 a week in only her second year in films) saw the casting couch as a passport to the west coast and Hollywood; and the mother of one future star is reliably said to have entered her bedroom with a carving knife in a final desperate attempt to persuade her daughter not to make for the modern Babylon.

The chorus girl was glamourised by Hollywood itself in a series of musical films like *Queen of the Chorus*, *The Gold Diggers of Broadway* and *Sally of the Scandals*. Nazimova, Mae Murray, Bebe Daniels, Pola Negri and Gloria Swanson all played girls from the chorus-line who eventually made good; and the films had an enormous effect on impressionable audiences . . . Joan Crawford's personable chorus girl in *Our Dancing Daughters* (1928) moved one high-school girl to write: 'I believe that nothing will happen to the carefree girl like Joan Crawford but it is the quiet girl who is always getting into trouble and making trouble.' That schoolgirl's mother, reading about Fatty Arbuckle's Orgy and the nude swimming parties in the back gardens of Hollywood may have felt somewhat differently.

The man who really built up the chorus on-screen, who taught the camera how to look at girls, was Busby Berkeley, director of a marvellous series of musicals from *Whoopee* (1930) to *Jumbo* (1962).

Berkeley's first great success was with a chorus of men of the 312th Field Artillery of the 79th Division of the US Army in France in 1917. He devised a system by which they could perform elaborate drill movements on a parade ground without audible orders from their officers. His success was so considerable that his system became a top military secret. After the war, back in America, came a number of years during which he gradually built up a career as an actor and director, particularly of musicals. He caused a sensation in *Seduction*, when on a stage covered in sand, he persuaded eight chorus girls to appear as nearly nude as any dancing-girl had ever appeared in America before 1924. In 1928, he choreographed five Broadway musicals, without ever having taken a dancing lesson; his sense of rhythm was impeccable, and so was his sense of the unusual—he got girls whose dancing experience was often extremely thin to perform very difficult routines.

'The first act of *Present Arms*' (wrote a critic in *The New York Times* in 1928) 'contains complicated and subtle rhythms that many a trained musician or a trained artist dancer would find next to impossible to perform. In many cases the girls are required to execute contrary rhythms, and in one number they are called upon to perform simultaneously two rhythms counter to each other, and also the music. A musical director who worked with Berkeley is quoted as saying that he did not dare to watch the dancing, for fear he could not move his baton to the required beat of the score . . . He creates none of these dances in advance; in fact, his inspiration seems to come from having the girls in front of him on the stage ready for work.'

Berkeley indeed seems always to have been particularly inspired by the ladies of the chorus: while he treated his stars well, he let the camera linger lovingly on the girls, giving fifty, eighty, a hundred of them almost a single luscious body.

In spring, 1930, Berkeley was introduced to Sam Goldwyn, who had bought the rights of *Whoopee*, a very successful Broadway show. 'He was very cordial, and said how happy he was to have me with him on his first musical venture,' Berkeley said later. 'He asked me what my first step would be, and I told him "Girls!"'

Berkeley always took great care in picking the girls for his musicals: beauty was by no means everything, for although many of Berkeley's most spectacular shots were relatively static, the girls all had to have the natural intelligence and quickness of mind to enable them to move together in complex, carefully choreographed routines. They also had to be strong as horses, for the long hours of rehearsal and shooting were killing in the early days before unionisation, even at $150 a week.

The Berkeley touch showed itself immediately in *Whoopee*. Goldwyn, watching the new director at work in the studio, was worried when he noticed Berkeley apparently concentrating much more than usual on the faces of individual girls. Why?, he asked. 'Well, we've got all these beautiful girls together—why not let the public see them properly?' asked Berkeley. The girls certainly did not object.

The obvious trade-mark of Berkeley's films was the geometrical patterns formed by his girls and photographed from above (he used

The Paramount Girls spell out the name of their employers; and (right) in The Kid from Spain **(1932) Busby Berkeley provided a touch of silhouetted nudity behind the screens**

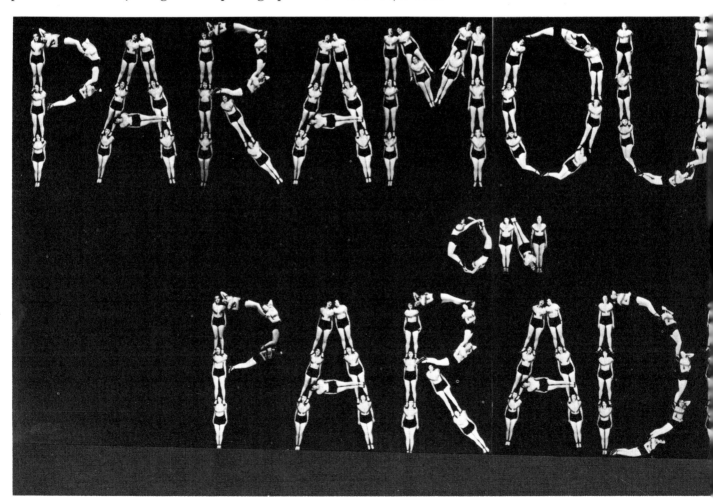

an overhead shot in his second film, *Palmy Days*, in 1931). In *The Kid from Spain* (1932), girls were laid out on the floor of the studio to form a living *tortilla* in a Spanish café!—and in the same film was a swimming-pool routine which was a foretaste of the dazzling scenes in Berkeley's great Esther Williams film *Million Dollar Mermaid* (1952).

Million Dollar Mermaid was one of the apotheoses of panache in Berkeley's career: the presence of Esther Williams meant that an all-swimming chorus would be necessary, and having provided himself with one, Berkeley used it with genius, and with an extravagance that lifts the eyebrows. There were a hundred girl and boy swimmers, who slid, standing, down 40-foot-high ramps into the water while carrying torches; twelve girls and boys simultaneously dived into the pool from twelve long swings, then made an elaborate star-shaped pattern in the water, and floated there smiling while Miss Williams dropped fifty feet into the middle of the star from a rope!

Despite his interest in the kind of uniformity and almost military precision which is now associated with, say, the Rockettes, Berkeley never allowed his routines to detract from the girls' sexuality. Sometimes he conveys this in long, lingering drifts of the camera over a harem of lovely ladies; sometimes by breaking the precision—as when, in *The Kid from Spain*, the Goldwyn Girls in swimsuits (and high-heeled shoes!) took their swimming-pool dip individually, while in the background behind ground-glass screens, shadowy and apparently naked girls dried themselves.

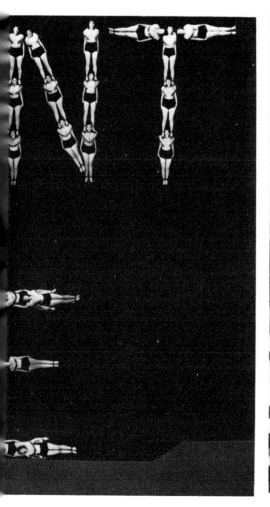

The sexuality broke through in the concerted numbers too: in *42nd Street*, for instance, the girls formed a living *meringue glacé*, frilly pants and headpieces making their naked backs even more enticing.

How the girls must have enjoyed themselves making Berkeley films —however hard he worked them! There was no question of their simply providing a backcloth to the action: they themselves were the stars of any Berkeley picture, and even when 55 of them were miming playing grand pianos, each felt important, as indeed she was. Time after time, a routine which should by now appear corny or *cliché*, impresses one, though it has been copied or imitated many times. Somehow, when the Goldwyn girls lined up in *Gold Diggers of 1937*, in white uniforms with flags and drums, it was not—still is not—just another chorus-girl military number: it is the essence of the Hollywood musical.

The emergence of the individual girl as a 'character' was slow, but (as in the theatre) inevitable. The effect of the vast crowd of girls, whether displayed in a living pattern or in a dance routine, palled, and gradually (especially as the big musical became prohibitively expensive)

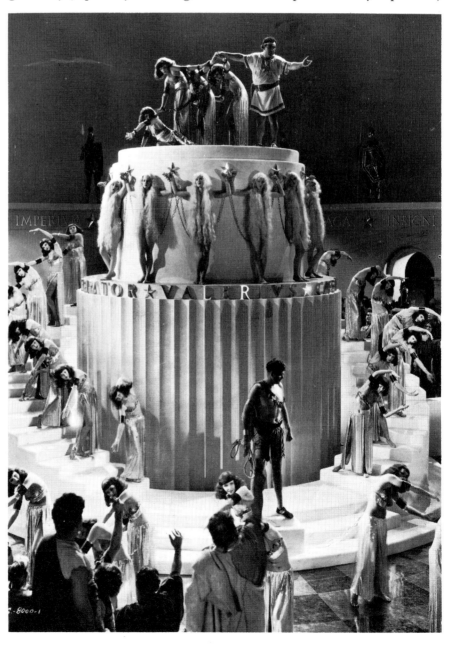

each girl became less a member of the chorus than an individual member of 'the crowd', which itself played a more important part than it once had. By the time *Meet Me in St Louis* was made in 1944, there was no chorus as such: the chorus was formed of individuals, members of a family, just as in the Judy Garland/Mickey Rooney musicals, the chorus consisted of the neighbourhood kids.

Techniques in dance, in the films, also improved out of all recognition: the dance sequences were properly choreographed, and it was no longer possible to present a row of kicking ladies or gentlemen as a serious contribution to even the most ordinary musical. Berkeley had put an end to all that. And now, as in *Seven Brides for Seven Brothers*, everybody sang, everybody danced, and there was often a small 'inner chorus' of particularly brilliant dancers to provide the main numbers. The big ballet sequences of, say, *An American in Paris* meant that 'chorus' could mean 'corps de ballet', while in the few big musicals still being made there is a fairly steady division between 'chorus' and 'extras'. As in the theatre, the old chorus seems to have gone for good.

Stills from two Busby Berkeley films. Left: apart from their wigs, the girls were nude in this scene from Roman Scandals (1933), which was filmed at night on a closed set! Right: Fifty-six little men under each of 56 grand pianos moved them about in a waltz-scene from Gold Diggers of 1935. The girls were drilled to conceal the men's legs with their long skirts!

171

'Often we'd audition
hundreds, and pick none.
"She's a bit heavy in the
thighs," we'd say, or
"a bit skimpy at the
shoulders", or "don't
much like her nose . . .""

Osborn Whitaker

9 **Dancers on Television**

Radio could not, of course, have been expected to play an important rôle in this story—though there were The Radio Dancers before the war, tapping out their routines in a BBC studio, in the tradition of the gramophone records offering 'the actual sound of Fred Astaire dancing.'

Television, however, is another matter. There, particularly in the late 1950s, was obviously the direction in which to look for any new development in chorus-work.

British television had got off to a bad start. There was only vestigial chorus-dancing in the brief television experiments before the war, and immovable cameras limited the technique unbearably. After the BBC's service was re-started in the late 1940s, photographed stage shows for some time continued to occupy the screen. The first notable break-though was in 1957, when George Inns mounted the first *Black and White Minstrel Show* at the Earl's Court Radio Show—and it was televised.

Mr Inns had always wanted to produce a minstrel show, ever since he had worked as an assistant to John Sharman and Harry Pepper on the radio *Kentucky Minstrels' Show*. George Mitchell, whose choirs had had great success on radio and television, trained a group of singers; the boys were 'blacked up', like the 'nigger minstrels' of the traditional concert variety shows of the first half of the century, and the girls 'added a touch of glamour'. (It ought to be said that there was not, nor has ever been, any real colour prejudice attached to the conception of these shows: no more prejudice at least than attaches to the traditional dumb Irishman or sly Cockney of traditional music-hall, or the idea of Mr Punch as a man with a hump-back).

The first *Minstrel Show*, with twelve girls and twelve boys, was an enormous success, and the following year there was a series of them, equally popular. In 1960 the show was put on the stage, and had an unprecedented success.

The great novelty of the show was in its perfected musical numbers: it did not rely on a small choir and a number of set dances. For the stage show, the producers copied the television (and of course film) technique of pre-recording a sound-track to which the company mimed, thus allowing far freer movement and far more advanced choreography than would have been possible if dancers had been asked to sing and move at the same time.

The producers have never entirely cheated: it would of course be easy to provide a magnificent sound-track recorded by a professional choir, and to get the performers to mime to that. But in fact all the dancers who appeared to be singing on-stage were in fact singing when the recording was made. There was a split within the chorus, in that the Mitchell Maids bore the main brunt of the singing; the Television Toppers, forming the other half of the female chorus, sang, but were not specially chosen for that purpose. The men were mainly singers, but though they were not professionally trained dancers, had to be able to cope with fairly advanced dance movement.

The result of all this was that the speed which was the essence of the television production was maintained in the theatre—and so was the sound quality of the voices (though in practice the sound was often very much over-amplified, as is the pernicious habit with stage musicals at the present time). The Black and White Minstrel Shows were the first to adopt this technique on a large scale.

The fact that the *Black and White Minstrel Show* is basically a chorus-show (though with its own stars, who have often emerged from the chorus) means that it is an arduous one for the singers and dancers: there have been as many as a hundred musical numbers in one show. The boys and girls have to be able to read music, or at least to be able to follow a 'top line.'

As with the Ziegfeld shows, or any popular show, the success of the Minstrels meant that a great number of girls—whether or not they could sing—applied for auditions. Apart from the fact that it was highly advisable that they should have some sort of a voice, there were few

Below, left: Windmill Girls went out to Alexandra Palace in 1946 to appear in one of the earliest BBC Television variety shows. Right, top: Even earlier —bathing beauties in a TV studio in 1933. Centre: 'I Want to Be a Chorus Girl' on TV in 1947 was a backstage feature. Bottom: The Television Toppers (1951)

Overleaf: The Black and White Minstrel Show: **(Top)** in 1964, and **(Bottom)** on-stage at the Victoria Palace in 1962

other constraints: it was preferable that they should be between 5 ft. 5 in. and 5 ft. 7 in. or thereabouts, but otherwise only the usual prerequisite of a trim figure and a pretty face applied.

Osborn Whitaker, who attended many auditions, pointed out that even if there were relatively few 'rules' for discovering a new member of the team, this by no means meant that it was easy. At auditions all over the country, he and a ballet-mistress would listen to and look at the contestants, and select them for a final audition in London.

'But often we would audition hundreds, and pick none. "She's a bit heavy in the thighs", we'd say, or "a bit skimpy at the shoulders", or "don't much like her nose . . ." Dreadful things to say about a girl, but we say them.'

The Mitchell Maids are perhaps more difficult to find than the Toppers: the latter only have to be dancers who can at least look as though they are singing well; the Maids have to be able to sing well, but must also have Topper figures and charm. A plain girl with the most beautiful voice has, alas, no chance.

Before a stage show, two weeks are spent on the music alone: there will be four days learning the music of the first half, then a day's recording; the following week, the same routine will be followed to produce a tape of the second half of the show. Television productions are handled at much greater speed, for reasons of studio availability and expense. Unsurprisingly, the boys and girls receive rather higher fees than a chorus would normally command.

Perhaps because the show is such an intense experience for its cast, the 'family' atmosphere pervades it even more than usual; there have been at least twenty marriages between members of the company, and the management has lost count of the number of small Toppers and Minstrels who have been born.

The success of *The Black and White Minstrel Show* partly rests on the music, which everyone knows and can sing along with, but partly too on the fact that all the girls are readily identified as 'the girl next door'— a great change from the days when the girls from the chorus were, or seemed, unattainable, even if in practice it proved otherwise. After a provincial tour in 1960, the show opened at the Victoria Palace, London (which has a tradition of fine choruses) in May 1962, and ran for over 4,000 performances before over five and a half million people, only coming off for another edition which had a similar success.

The most interesting recent development in 'choral dancing'—if that phrase continues to have any meaning—came in BBC Television in 1967, when Stewart Morris, Head of BBC Television Light Entertainment, 'invented' a new group for a television variety show built around the Australian entertainer Rolf Harris.

'I had been looking for some time for a new way of presenting dancing on television,' he says. 'When I started in television, the dancers came from the theatre, and one's job as a producer was to try to move the theatre into television. Even to this day

when they engage television floor managers, they ask
"What theatrical experience do you have?" I always
find this worrying, because I think television by now
should have its own technique, and teach its own
technique.

'I was presented with the problem of Rolf Harris,
who was not a sex symbol, and was known in this
country basically as a children's entertainer. I wanted
to keep his children's audience, and yet make him
attractive to adults, and the simplest way of doing that
seemed to me to be to surround him with young people.

'I had tried one "special" with an Italian singer,
when I used 36 teenagers who had no professional
teaching whatsoever; it didn't in my opinion come off—
they were too raw, and could not respond quickly
enough. So now I advertised, I telephoned every
school in the country, I should think, and I auditioned
between 2,500 and 3,000 youngsters.'

The Young Generation, the team of dancers which was the result of
the experiment, is far from being 'a chorus' in the old sense of the term.
It is, however, highly professional; though the dancer may be in her
first job, she has certainly had a professional training. She is paid more
than the Equity minimum, and deserves it; the work is very hard,
while the group is working (and it is engaged by television for the run
of a show, usually for thirteen performances). There are four days in
which to learn the routines for a single television spectacular, and each
show can have as many as eight routines.

The freshness and newness of The Young Generation, which caught
on immediately with the audience, is—as with the Black and White
Minstrels—identity with a familiar image. The audience, even of
middle-aged or elderly people, can see themselves in the young people
on the screen, partly because they have broken away from the tradition
of the chorus, and appear simply to be kids having a good time.

Each individual in the team is carefully chosen by Mr Morris himself. Everyone must have at least a basic dancing ability—someone with
a classical background, the right appearance and personality, who is at
least not tone-deaf, has a chance. The musical director for the group,
Alan Ainsworth, has been known to produce a voice out of a young
dancer who didn't know she possessed one. Most of the team end up
being able to sight-read music.

Mr Morris aimed always at a group of individuals: at a 'chorus' which
was in itself 'a star', though no individual was. There have never been
any strict physical requirements: there have been tall and short girls
and boys, and indeed rules as such seem noticeable mainly for their
absence.

'A girl obviously has to be attractive in some way,' says Mr Morris;
'she has to be beautiful, or pert, or pretty—she has to have *some* appeal.
There is no age limit; we've had several sixteen-year-olds, though the

current age probably averages nineteen or something like it, and there are one or two who've stayed on into their mid-twenties.'

The success of the group was so immediate that a crop of imitations sprung up, particularly in the US. But The Young Generation manages to remain unique; it frequently appears on television abroad, and has done stage-shows in England, including a Royal Command Variety Performance.

Its popularity has brought some problems. It became so well known that when one girl was wanted, at least 800 were auditioned, and then the girl wasn't found.

'When we held a second audition,' says Mr Morris, 'at a place called Putney Ballroom, I drove my car round the corner and thought there was a riot—I couldn't get near the building. When I got into the ballroom, I had to stand on a chair in order to see the kids—they were packed in, at least half of them with their mothers, who had come to protect their children, all standing there with their rolled umbrellas.'

Many of the youngsters were under a misapprehension: they thought that what was wanted was gogo dancers or disco dancers; and when a routine was set by a choreographer for them to learn, they had an instant fit of the horrors.

The Young Generation are not a copy of anything that has gone before them. They are a creation of television for television, and the small screen will never be the same again, as far as chorus-dancing is concerned.

The Young Generation filming for TV on the set of the musical film Oliver, **in 1972**

Les Girls...?

Left: The chorus girls in Universal's film Parole! were all convicts, entertaining their fellows. 'Real' drag artists are more serious and better-looking, though often as obviously male. Left, below: The cast of Splinters, an ex-servicemen's company popular between the wars. Below: A 1967 all-male pantomime chorus. Bottom: Boys at the Casino de Paris

10 Today—and Tomorrow!

The history of the chorus girl is ending not with a bang, but a whimper. Anyone who now reads Emily Soldene's description of the entertainments at the Empire, the Palace, the Alhambra in the 1890s can only be filled with nostalgia:

'The gorgeous, luxurious appointments of the
English houses, the light, the gleam and sparkle,
and the gay *abandon* of the audience, the magnitude
of the entertainment and the ballet!—the ballet
crowded with the most beautiful girls in the world,
dressed in abbreviated costumes, designed by the
finest artists of Europe, dancing to an immense
band of splendid musicians . . .'

It all now seems unbearably enviable. In England, the chorus spluttered out in the days when television was making its first impact, and the small screen began to keep people at home in front of their sets rather than out at the theatre taking part in the kind of entertainment their fathers and grandfathers enjoyed. Anyone who remembers the 'tatty tours' (as the girls themselves describe them) of the late 1940s and early 1950s will do so with a shudder: in a last-minute attempt to lure people back to the theatres, managements sent out around the provinces really awful little sex shows (reminiscent of American burlesque) in which the sleasiest strippers performed to badly pre-recorded music or a tiny, raucous band, while a small chorus jogged about behind them.

This was the nadir of the chorus-girl story: crouched over a pan of 'wet-white' mixed by the head girl, and plastering it on their legs and bodies while the rain came in through the roof of the draughty dressing-room, they must all have regretted the day they first thought of 'going on the stage.' Life, as this book has perhaps shown, was never particularly glamorous back-stage—and certainly not in terms of salary. By 1938 the wage had only risen to £3 a week for the back row of the chorus, and even in the 1950s was not much better. The desperately awful revues which toured the provinces in the two decades after the war were designed to rescue the living theatre; but they only pushed it more firmly under, and held it there. Theatres all over the country turned over to wrestling, films, became bingo halls, or just simply closed down.

By the time the public had got used to television, and showed signs of beginning to turn back to the theatre, expenses of production had risen so steeply that the staging of a really luxuriant and ambitious musical or revue (revue was virtually dead by now, anyway) had become impracticable.

The fact that the virtual disappearance of the large chorus from the stage has really little to do with any change of public taste, was amply demonstrated by the 1970s revival of *No, No, Nanette* in New York—a show in which the chorus stole much of the generous applause. The farsighted producers realised that the current appetite for nostalgia might support an expensive revival of one of the most popular musicals of 1925, and engaged Busby Berkeley to supervise it.

*'a pretty girl who
naked is
is worth a million
statues.'*

e. e. cummings

The chorus of Hair (this is the London cast) were individuals who happened to be on-stage at the same time; the lack of discipline was total—boys and girls even chose to strip or not to strip, as the mood took them, from night to night

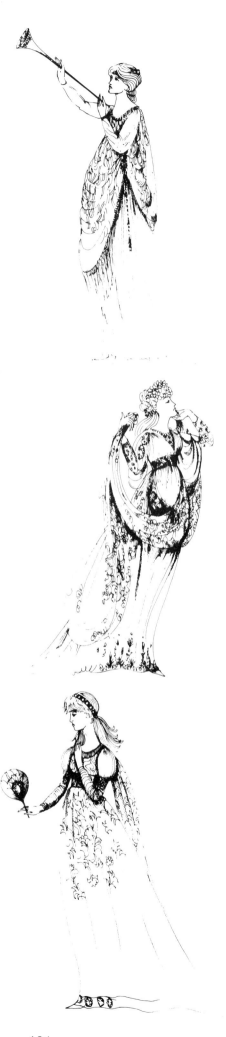

Successful though it was, the revival proved once again the vulnerability of the chorus-girls' life. Cyma Rubin, the producer, whose experience of show-business certainly eschewed any romantic attitudes, paid off a number of girls (who she considered 'dogs') while the show was still on tour—it cost her $5,000 to do so. Even while waiting to go into New York, after a brilliant success out of town, one boy slightly taller than the others in the chorus was pulled out of a queue at an airport and told: 'Here's your two weeks' pay and $22 for a 'plane ticket back to New York.' A rather shorter dancer had been found.

Recent London musicals have notably failed to provide a chorus of any dimensions: a spoof of the 'twenties musical films in *Billy Liar* at Drury Lane, which merited a dancing chorus of 30 tail-coated men and beautiful women, scraped by on very few; and when a traditional chorus *is* engaged for a show, the old atmosphere and verve seem to have vanished. *Cinderella*, a very traditional pantomime mounted for Twiggy in London at Christmas 1974, had its chorus of boys and girls (the Prince was, against tradition, a man, and had male dancers to support him); they were well-costumed and enthusiastic, but something of their frivolity and simple joy had gone, and what was left was a rather selfconscious group of dancers who seemed hardly to grasp what their purpose was.

There was also a small chorus of children, again traditional in pantomime—and the *Cinderella* kids included one spectacular example of the typically nauseating 'theatrical' child making a dead set at stealing the hearts of the audience, and succeeding only in turning its stomach.

The provocative chirpiness of the children has contributed to pantomime in the past, and will no doubt continue to do so as long as that strange form of entertainment continues. The chorus kid often grew almost inevitably into the chorus girl.

Conditions for children working in the theatre are now of course strictly supervised, whether they are appearing in panto or as *Neibelungen* in *Das Rhinegold* (the Royal Opera House in London in fact uses 'ordinary' schoolchildren, given a pleasant opportunity to taste life back-stage). In general, the children come from small schools which concentrate on 'stage dancing' (in the provinces) or from the acknowledged stage schools in the large cities. They must be versatile, with the means to 'put over a number', and in fact are often miniature chorus girls—with the exception that the law keeps a strict eye on them, demanding for instance that they are out of the theatre by a specified time (which is why they are so often missing from the final walk-down).

The pantomime child always used to have her eyes on the chorus as an ultimate, or penultimate, ambition: she would now be extremely unwise to do so, not only because the number of girls able to find work has shrunk significantly, but because a qualified secretary has not only better security but a far better salary. Equity, the British actors' trade union, has worked out forms of contract which aim at safeguarding the chorus: but these still by no means provide for ideal conditions of work, though they would have rejoiced the heart of the girl of the 1880s.

The chorus contract for London musical plays, for instance, sets out

A scene from the English National Opera production of Gilbert & Sullivan's Patience, and (opposite) some of John Stoddart's costume designs

a minimum salary of £36 a week for a once-nightly show, rising to £39 for twice-nightly, and making allowance for extra payment to the Head Chorister. There must also be payment of £34 a week for rehearsals—not too long ago, there was no pay at all during rehearsals—and a touring allowance of £9 a week for pre-London try-outs.

There are also, of course, agreements for resident seasons at provincial theatres (a minimum salary of £30 a week for everyone with previous theatrical experience, and £25 for newcomers; the same rates apply to provincial tours), and for overseas engagements (which among other things make such necessary provision for emergencies as the deposit with Equity of a sum to cover two weeks' salary for every girl engaged, to cover the event of a production 'folding').

Even with managements working under the handicap of having to pay the girls reasonable salaries, there is no doubt that the old alchemy could still work (as it did on Broadway with *No, No, Nanette*). Recent attempts have failed for all sorts of reasons.

One which seemed likely to succeed was the *Royalty Folies* staged by Paul Raymond in London in 1974. No expense was spared to mount a London equivalent of an old-style Paris revue which would have the added advantage (the producer believed) of making use of the relaxed censorship laws to bring total nudity to the stage—and after all, *Oh, Calcutta!* was having an apparently interminable run, and *The Dirtiest Show in Town*, which depended solely on beautiful young people displaying their bodies in sexual situations, had run well.

**The 'Diddy-Men' ensemble
from** The Royalty Follies, **1974**

The programme was carefully planned—including big staged musical numbers, a Genghis Khan number catering for those interested in mild flagellation, and a none-too-subtle skit on the James Bond films in which nude girls surrounded a somewhat coy young gentleman who once divested of his drawers spent most of his time devising ways in which he could remain resolutely facing up-stage!

The girls too were obviously carefully-chosen to appeal to every taste: there were tall girls, shorter girls, plump girls and thin girls, black girls, white girls, Chinese girls and girls—no doubt—from Neasden and Stoke-on-Trent. They were all beautiful; they were divided into strictly observed categories—The Royalty Girls, The Nude Dancers, The Nude Showgirls—knew their places and stayed in them.

So what went wrong? Partly the choreography, insufficiently inventive, and partly the costumes—for the designer was faced with apparently insuperable difficulty: as Erté and Alec Shanks and others had shown, it was possible to design the most beautiful costumes for girls whose breasts only were to be bared; but when the pubic area has almost compulsarily to be displayed, costumes have to be bunched around the waist and legs and arms—the only part of the body left!—resulting in a general shape which can be nothing but ugly.

The nude dancers have other problems. As nude ballet had already shown, nudes who dance are not always able to remain seriously beautiful. The art of the dance is the art of muscular control, and there are some areas of the human body, in both men and women, not susceptible to muscular control. When the dancer stops, they go on moving, and the effect is irresistably comic. (Comedy in fact was once brilliantly used, in an amazingly vulgar but hysterically funny sketch in which the girls wore immense false heads which came to their waists, with their breasts forming eyes and their nipples, the pupils.)

There are some areas of the chorus-girls' history which we have not

touched on: there is the skating chorus girl, for instance, who takes part in the ice extravaganzas now increasingly common. Here is an often very large chorus, possible because the conditions of an ice-show allow a producer to save on scenery what he can spend on salaries and costumes. Ice-choreography is enormously influenced by the theatre, and the girls and boys have work to do which reminds one irresistibly of the great days of the chorus.

Then there are the more outrageous *ensembles* on the very edge of any definition of 'a chorus'—the all-male chorus of the drag show *Splinters*, for instance, which consisted entirely of ex-servicemen, and was known in France as *Les Rouges et Noirs*. At the London Coliseum, in 1920, the men in their bobbed hair and with their boyish figures were in the height of female fashion, and looked exactly like a chorus of beautiful, elegant young girls. Then, with the Second World War, came *Soldiers in Skirts*, *Misleading Ladies*, *Forces in Petticoats* . . . More recent drag shows have starred individuals, such as the inimitable Danny la Rue, who have never surrounded themselves with drag choruses.

But we have gone too far. Whether the history of the chorus-girl has ended, except for the brilliant pockets of resistance in Paris and Las Vegas, only time will tell. The old-style Girl, whose purpose was simply to stand around and be admired, *has* probably gone for ever. Now, when we see a group of beautiful girls in a theatre, we demand that they *do* something rather than just stand there—Miss World contests provide the proper forum, these days, for the beautiful dumb blonde insufficiently accomplished to be really entertaining.

Economics may forbid the kind of large-scale show which once most commonly employed the Chorus Girl—but while men (and women) continue to enjoy looking at women, it is doubtful whether she will vanish completely and permanently from the theatre scene. And surely it would be a sad day when she did.

Bibliography

Agate, James: *Immoment Toys* (London 1945)

Barton Baker, H.: *History of the London Stage* (London 1934)

Barker, Gabrielle: *Desert Angels* (London 1956)

Beerbohm, Max: *Around Theatres* (London 1953)

Booth, J. B.: *Life, Laughter and Brass Hats* (London 1939)

Damase, Jacques: *Les Folies du Music-Hall* (Paris 1960)

Derval, Paul: *Folies Bergère* (Paris 1954)

Dunn, Don: *The Making of No, No, Nanette* (New Jersey 1972)

Engel, Lehman: *The American Musical Theater* (New York 1967)

Farnsworth, Marjorie: *The Ziegfeld Follies* (London 1956)

Forbes-Winslow, D. *Daly's* (London 1944)

Foster, George: *The Spice of Life* (London ?1930)

Green, Stanley: *The World of Musical Comedy* (London 1968)

Guest, Ivor: *The Ballet of the Second Empire* (London 1955)

———: *Victorian Ballet-Girl* (London 1957)

Hanson, Lawrence and Elizabeth: *The Tragic Life of Toulouse-Lautrec* (London 1956)

Hibbert, H. G.: *A Playgoer's Memories* (London 1920)

Howard, J. Bannister: *50 Years a Showman* (London 1938)

Kobal, John: *Gotta Sing Gotta Dance* (London 1971)

MacQueen-Pope, W.: *Gaiety, Theatre of Enchantment* (London: 1949)

Mander, Raymond and Mitchenson, Joe: *Musical Comedy* (London 1969)

———: *Revue* (London 1971)

Mason, Rupert (ed.): *Roses of Thespis* (London 1928)

Rosen, Marjorie: *Popcorn Venus* (New York 1973)

Scott, Clement (ed. and others): *The Theatre* (London: 1879–)

Shaw, Bernard: *Our Theatre in the Nineties* (London 1932)

Short, Ernest: *Sixty Years of the Theatre* (London 1951)

Short, Ernest and Compton-Rickett, Arthur: *Ring up the Curtain* (London 1938)

Sitwell, Osbert: *Left Hand! Right Hand!* (London 1945)
The Scarlet Tree (London 1946)

Smith, Albert: *Natural History of the Ballet Girl* (London 1847)

Soldene, Emily: *My Theatrical and Musical Recollections* (London 1897)

Thomas, Tony and Terry, Jim: *The Busby Berkeley Book* (London 1973)

Trollope, Frances: *Domestic Manners of the Americans* (London 1832)

van Damm, Vivian: *Tonight and Every Night* (London 1952)

'Walter', *My Secret Life* (London 1882)

Wilson, A. E.: *Christmas Pantomime* (London 1934)

Acknowledgements

We have received a great deal of help from chorus girls past and present, to whom we express our thanks. No book of this kind can be completed without reference to the omnipotent historians and scholars of theatre history, Raymond Mander and Joe Mitchenson, who have not only helped with photographs from their magnificent collection, but have recommended sources, and have saved us from some (though no doubt not all) errors of fact. Our thanks, too, go to Miss Bluebell and Peter Baker, her English manager; Osborn Whitaker (of Robert Luff Holdings Ltd.); Stewart Morris (Head of Television Light Entertainment, BBC); Peter Warren; Jean Canter; Vivienne Rane; Rita Croke; Kirk Crivello. As usual, the staffs of the British Museum Reading Room and of the London Library have been extremely helpful. Many thanks, too, go to Anne-Marie Erlich, an invaluable picture researcher.

We acknowledge the kind permission of the Society of Authors (on behalf of the Bernard Shaw estate) to quote from Shaw's theatre criticism; and of Sir Rupert Hart-Davis and Mrs Eva Reichmann for permission to quote from the criticism of Max Beerbohm. Messrs Chappell & Co. are the copyright holders of *The Darlings of the Chorus*.

Photo acknowledgements Roger Baker—*Drag* 181; Courtesy Bluebell Organisation 80, 98below, 115top; Courtesy Bluebell Organisation/photo Daniel Frasnay 48–9, 119, 122, 123, 126–7, 128below; BBC 172, 175top and mid, 179; Camera Press 175; Courtauld Institute/S.P.A.D.E.M. 36; Rita Croke 115; Bernard Delfont Organisation 128; English National Opera/photo Donald Southern 186below; Mary Evans Picture Library 10; Fox Photos 174–5; Grosvenor Gallery/photo Rodney Todd White 69, 136; Tom Hustler 151; Imperial War Museum 156below, 156top left; Kansas State Historical Society 84, 85; John Kobal Collection 76below, 77, 124–5, 160, 162below, 163, 168–9, 169, 170, 171; Robert Luff Holdings Ltd 176top and below; Mander and Mitchenson Theatre Collection 22–3, 24, 25, 30, 32–3, 50–1, 54, 54–5, 56, 57bottom left, 57bottom right, 58, 60, 61, 63, 66, 67, 69below, 70, 72, 73, 75, 82, 104, 106–7, 110, 111, 139, 141, 143, 144–5, 147, 152, 153; Mansell Collection 12, 13, 16–17, 19, 26, 32, 40–1; Morris Newcombe 182; New York Public Library 86, 88–9, 90, 91, 92, 93, 96, 97; Nottingham Museum and Art Gallery 27; Picturepoint 113; Julia Parker 108–9; Popperfoto 131, 186; Private collection 68; Radio City Music Hall 94; Radio Times Hulton Picture Library 20, 22, 28, 31, 33, 34, 38, 45, 46–7, 57, 70–1, 74, 98, 130, 131bottom, 132, 133top left, 133right, 134–5, 137, 140–1, 148, 149, 150–1, 152, 153bottom, 155, 157bottom left, back endpaper; Rex Features front endpapers, 80, 113, 118–19, 133bottom left, 154, cover; Barnet Saidman F.R.P.S., F.I.B.P. 76top, 116, 120middle; By Courtesy of Sotheby and Co. 8, 9; Victoria and Albert Museum/Enthoven Collection 65, 71; Reg Wilson 120–1above and below.

Index

The End